The Five Strategic Pillars Methodology: Empowering Leaders
to Build Businesses that Scale, Sustain, and Succeed
By Moe Nawaz

Publisher Information

Duke Brothers Ltd
1st Floor
One Mayfair Place
Mayfair
London E1J 8AJ
United Kingdom
Tel: +44 (0)207 516 1001

For additional resources, mentorship, and strategic insights from

Moe Nawaz, The Strategic Architect, please visit:

www.moenawaz.com

Table Of Contents

ACKNOWLEDGMENTS 2

ABOUT THE AUTHOR: MOE NAWAZ......................................4

INTRODUCTION — Before the Architecture, ...5

The Room Where No One Spoke..7
The 1% Advantage 8
Forty Years of Scars, Failures, and Structural Lessons 9
Why Leaders Call Me Only When Something Is Wrong........10
The Birth of the Five Pillars and the Missing Piece................11
An Invitation Into Structural Clarity 13

CHAPTER 1: The Day I Realised Architecture....................15

A Boardroom Full of Brilliant People and a Fracture 15
My First Major Failure as a Young Consultant 18
The Price of Effort Without Architecture 22
What This Book Will Help You Finally See..............................25

CHAPTER 2: The 3XV Strategic Engine™ 29

Vision: Designing the Destination..29
Value: Why the Market Chooses You or Leaves You...............35
Vehicle: The Engine That Carries Your Promise.....................41
When 3XV Is Wrong, Nothing Else Works...............................50

CHAPTER 3: Translating 3XV Into Architecture...............**57**

The Moment Strategy Meets Structure 57

Why Leaders Resist the Truth 63

The Hard Lesson of Being Early...69

CHAPTER 4: SYSTEMISATION, THE FLOW.................**75**

Why Flow Fails in Good Companies 75

The Hidden Weight of Invisible Decisions..............................79

How 3XV Shapes Your Systems 83

The Dubai Flow Misdiagnosis 87

Your First Structural Clarity Question....................................91

CHAPTER 5: Staffability, The People-Bearing Pillar...........**95**

People Do Not Fail, Architecture Fails Them 95

The Leadership Load I Ignored Until It Hurt Us...................101

How 3XV Determines Talent Structure.................................112

The Hiring Mistake That Cost Millions 117

CHAPTER 6: SCALABILITY, THE GROWTH................**121**

Why Eight-Figure Companies Hit Invisible Ceilings 121

Growth Is Not Scale 125

Why Your Vehicle Determines What Can Scale 131

My Biggest Scaling Misdiagnosis..137

The First Sign I Missed 139

The Turning Point That Followed 141

The Courage to Stop Scaling Bad Structure..........................143

CHAPTER 7: Sustainability, The Resilience............................ **147**

What Breaks First Under Pressure 147

The Drift I Did Not Catch in Time... 152

How 3XV Protects Long-Term Integrity................................. 156

Cultural Architecture and the Cost of Ignoring Truth 161

CHAPTER 8: Sellability, The Transfer-Bearing Pillar.........**167**

Every Business Is for Sale, Even When You Do..................... 167

The Silent Walk-Away Signals... 174

3XV in Due Diligence 177

Founder Dependency, The Silent Killer of Value.................. 183

CHAPTER 9: Diagnosing the Pillars Through the 3.......... **189**

The Day I Found the Fracture No One Else Saw 189

3XV as a Diagnostic Compass 194

The Pillar Baseline Assessment.. 201

CHAPTER 10: Designing Your Architecture Blueprint......**209**

Choosing the Right Pillar to Strengthen First 209

Trade-Offs, Pain Points, and Tough Calls 215

The Three-Year Architecture Plan 221

CHAPTER 11: Operating Rhythm, The Enforcement.........**227**

Why Architecture Drifts Without Rhythm 227

The Week, Month, Quarter Cadence 235

CHAPTER 12: Compression, Turning Five-Year 243

The First Time I Compressed a CEO's Timeline 243

Why 3XV Plus the Pillars Make Compression Possible 250

A Three-Year Compression Case Study 258

CHAPTER 13: When to Call a Strategic Architect 265

The Fear, Instinct, and Gut Tension Before They Call..........................265

Why Leaders Do Not See the Fracture................................272

Selective Work, Deep Impact 278

CHAPTER 14: Your First Ninety Days of 285

Your 3XV Reset..285

Your Pillar Baseline..290

Your First Structural Move..297

A Personal Request From the..305

ACKNOWLEDGMENTS

For those who shaped the architect, and strengthened the architecture.

My first and deepest gratitude is to the Almighty. Whatever insight, clarity, or structural intelligence you find in these pages began long before my pen touched paper. The design behind my life, the drift, the load, the failures, the unexpected openings, was never mine alone. I have simply tried to build with what I was shown, one quiet revelation at a time.

To my family: thank you for being the supporting beams behind this work. You carried the unseen weight, the late nights, the silent thinking, the weekends turned into whiteboard sessions, without complaint and without ever asking for credit. If this book holds any architectural strength, it is because you held the structure around me.

To my mentors and teachers, Jay Abraham, Peter Drucker, W. Edwards Deming, Ray Dalio, Ben Gay III, Drayton Bird, and Eliyahu M. Goldratt, you gave me not answers but discipline. You taught me to follow the thread beneath behaviour, to trust structure over noise, and to treat clarity as a moral obligation. Your fingerprints sit quietly inside these pages.

To my clients, from FTSE 100 and Fortune 500 boardrooms to the relentless founders across Europe, the Middle East, Asia, and North America, thank you for inviting me into the rooms where the real work happens. Not the rooms staged for presentations and press releases, but the private ones where fear, ambition, responsibility, and truth coexist. The architecture in this book was shaped inside those crucible moments.

To the men and women of the Directors' WarRoom, you are living proof that elite leadership can be disciplined without being rigid, powerful without being loud, and ambitious without drifting into chaos. Your willingness to confront uncomfortable truths continues to refine my thinking. Many of the stories, insights, and structural frameworks in this book were forged in conversation with you.

And to you, the reader, whether you lead a £20M company or are navigating the transition into the 8– or 9–figure arena, thank you for choosing architecture over adrenaline. You already carry enough pressure, expectation, and responsibility. The fact that you chose to spend your time with this work tells me something important:
you are building not for today, but for tomorrow.

If you wish to understand the deeper ethos behind the Directors' WarRoom and the design of high-trust, high-performance environments, you can explore it further in *Mastermind Groups: The Fastest & Safest Way to Grow Your Business – The Directors WarRoom Edition*, available on Amazon.

But for now, the blueprint begins here.
Build with intention.
Scale with intelligence.
Lead beyond yourself.

With respect and resolve,
Moe Nawaz

ABOUT THE AUTHOR: MOE NAWAZ

The Strategic Architect to FTSE 100 Boards and High-Growth CEOs

Moe Nawaz is recognised globally as The Strategic Architect, a structural thinker who helps leaders redesign the internal architecture of their organisations for clarity, flow, resilience, and scale. His work happens behind closed doors, inside the private rooms where decisions carry weight, failure is expensive, and leadership cannot hide.

For more than four decades, Moe has advised FTSE 100 boards, sovereign-backed institutions, and high-growth CEOs across Europe, the Middle East, Asia, and North America. He is not a public figure by design. His influence lives in the results of the leaders he guides, the companies rebuilt, the cultures recalibrated, and the systems that continue to operate long after he leaves the room.

Founders and boards bring Moe into their most sensitive moments for one reason:he sees the architecture beneath the performance.
Where others see symptoms, he sees structure.
Where others see speed, he sees load.
Where others see success, he sees drift quietly forming beneath the surface.

His proprietary frameworks, including the Five Strategic Pillars® (Systemisation, Staffability, Scalability, Sustainability, Sellability), have become the structural foundation for thousands of organisations seeking clarity, intelligent scale, and long-term transferability. But while the pillars guide the operational structure, Moe's deeper contribution lies in what he calls Architectural Leadership, the discipline of designing leaders, decisions, and organisations that can survive themselves.

Moe is also the founder of the Directors' WarRoom, an invitation-only mastermind for elite CEOs who choose pressure, accountability, and intelligent design over ego and noise. Inside the WarRoom, leaders compress five-year goals into three, not by working harder but by working structurally, through architecture, AI-enabled systems, and disciplined execution.

His journey did not begin in boardrooms.
Moe left school at sixteen with no qualifications.
He was fired twenty-seven times, and rehired twenty-two, by executives who weren't ready to hear the structural truths he saw before they did. When reality eventually caught up with their organisations, those same leaders brought him back, often with apology letters and bonus cheques they never expected to write.

Those scars became the foundation for the thinking in this book.

Behind the scenes, Moe continues to mentor the next generation of founders, advise governments and global organisations on structural transformation, and speak internationally on leadership architecture, organisational resilience, and the future of enterprise in the age of AI.

To explore private mentoring, the Directors' WarRoom, or additional Strategic Architect tools and frameworks, visit: www.MoeNawaz.com

INTRODUCTION — Before the Architecture, There Is the Truth

The Room Where No One Spoke

I walked into that boardroom expecting clarity. Twelve leaders, a £100M plus organisation, a strategy session scheduled months in advance. Everything about the environment signalled confidence. Their reports were polished, their numbers strong, their faces composed. On the surface, it looked like a company on the rise, secure, ambitious, proud of its momentum.

And yet, the moment I stepped inside, something felt wrong.

There's a particular kind of silence that doesn't belong in a healthy organisation. It isn't the quiet of focus or discipline. It's the quiet of avoidance, of things felt but not spoken. That was the silence hanging in the air that morning. Heavier than the agenda. Louder than the voices that would follow. A silence that carried the weight of something these leaders already sensed but hadn't allowed themselves to name.

They spoke, of course. People always do. Updates, wins, projections, targets. Everything sounded sensible. But the rhythm was off. Their sentences felt rehearsed, their enthusiasm strained. Even their smiles were a little too fixed. Success on paper has a shine to it, but when the architecture underneath begins to drift, the shine becomes brittle.

I scanned the room quietly, not for words but for weight. The COO avoided eye contact. The CFO kept adjusting her chair as if she couldn't settle. The CEO, usually commanding, had a stillness that felt more like fatigue than confidence. No one interrupted. No one challenged. No one asked the difficult questions strong leadership teams usually embrace without hesitation.

It was as if the company was holding its breath.

I've learned, through four decades in boardrooms across the world, that this is how organisational breakdown first introduces itself, not with chaos, not with firefighting, but with a subtle shift in the atmosphere. When leaders feel something they cannot quite articulate, the room tells the truth long before the numbers do.

That morning, I realised I wasn't listening to their words. I was listening to the pressure underneath them.

They didn't know it yet, but something fundamental in their architecture had already begun to crack.

And this, this moment of unspoken truth, is where my real work always begins.

The 1% Advantage

Whenever I sit with a leadership team for the first time, I tell them something that instantly lowers the temperature in the room:

"You know ninety-nine percent more about your business than I ever will."

And it's true.

They've lived the early struggles, the late nights, the product failures, the difficult hires, the market shifts. They carry the history, the instincts, and the emotional memory of decisions that shaped the organisation. They know the people, the processes, the clients, the risks. They know the ninety-nine percent that can only be earned through experience.

But it's the remaining one percent that changes everything.

My work has never been about knowing more. It has been about seeing what others don't, or can't, because they're standing too close to the structure they built. After forty years of working with leaders across industries, continents, and economic cycles, patterns emerge. Not surface-level patterns, deep architectural ones. The kind that reveal where pressure accumulates, where alignment is slipping, and where the future is being shaped quietly, beneath the noise of daily operations.

That one percent is not genius. It's not brilliance. It's not some mystical insight.
It's repetition, scar tissue, and pattern recognition earned the long, painful way.

Leaders often mistake motion for progress, and progress for strength. My role is to help them see the architecture underneath their movement, the design that holds everything together or, sometimes, the design that quietly limits everything they're trying to achieve.

When I share the one percent idea, leaders usually lean back, exhale, and let their guard drop. Because deep down, they already know something isn't aligned. They've felt the hesitation, the drift, the slip in rhythm, but without a name for it, they keep pushing harder, hoping effort will fix what only architecture can solve.

This book is built around that one percent.

Not the ninety-nine you already know, but the unseen truth that will change how you view your organisation forever.

Forty Years of Scars, Failures, and Structural Lessons

When people meet me today, they often see the calm, measured Strategic Architect who helps leaders rebuild the structure of their organisations. What they don't see is the four decades of scars that shaped that clarity. My understanding of architecture wasn't born from classrooms or consultants, it was carved out of mistakes, misreadings, and the painful consequences of believing effort could compensate for structural truth.

In my early years, I thought intelligence and determination were enough. I believed that if I worked harder than everyone else, kept moving, kept pushing, kept solving, I could force a company into strength. But organisations don't bend to effort. They bend to design. And I learned that lesson the hard way.

I remember one engagement, a company expanding faster than its structure could carry. I encouraged the acceleration, mistaking momentum for readiness. When the architecture buckled, good people paid the price. That failure left a permanent mark on me. It taught me that enthusiasm without structure is dangerous, and confidence without clarity is a liability.

Over the years, those lessons multiplied. In some companies, I spoke truths too early, truths leaders weren't ready to hear. I was fired for it twenty-seven times. And then rehired twenty-two times within three years by the same leaders who eventually realised those early truths were not criticism, but warnings. That experience taught me another structural lesson: timing matters as much as accuracy. A truth spoken too early can cause as much damage as a truth spoken too late.

Those scars sharpened my instincts. They taught me to look beneath the surface, to listen to the pressure rather than the words, and to respect the limits of any system, including my own.

If I speak with authority today, it is only because failure taught me what success never could: that architecture always wins, effort always exhausts, and truth eventually demands to be seen.

Why Leaders Call Me Only When Something Is Wrong

Leaders don't call me when things are going well. They call when something feels off, even when the numbers say everything is fine. It rarely starts with a crisis. More often, it begins with a subtle shift they can't quite articulate. A hesitation in meetings. A drift in priorities. A sense that the organisation is moving, but not necessarily progressing.

They can feel the pressure, but they can't locate the source.

When leaders reach out, they're not looking for motivation. They're not looking for a consultant to tidy up processes or run workshops. They're looking for someone who sees what they can't, someone who can walk into a room and sense the fracture beneath the surface. That fracture might be in decision flow, leadership load, cultural integrity, misaligned incentives, or a pillar beginning to carry more weight than it was designed for.

What brings them to me is not panic, it's instinct.

Many admit, quietly, "Something isn't right, but I don't know what it is." And that honesty is where our work begins. In fact, some leaders have asked me to sign agreements preventing me from helping their competitors, not out of fear of losing secrets, but fear that my ability to pinpoint the fracture could give someone else an advantage.

That tension speaks to the nature of the work. I am called when silence grows heavier than data. When the architecture starts drifting before the symptoms appear. When the organisation is still standing, but the load-bearing truth has begun to shift.

And sometimes, another foreshadow from my past, I'm called only after the truth I once spoke too early finally makes itself impossible to ignore. Leaders who once dismissed the warning later return, realising that the fracture was always there; they just didn't have the language to see it.

My work begins where instinct ends, at the exact point where the organisation starts whispering what everyone else has learned to ignore.

The Birth of the Five Pillars and the Missing Piece

The Five Strategic Pillars did not arrive in a single moment of brilliance. They emerged slowly, painfully, through years of watching good companies collapse under the weight of their own success. I kept seeing the same fractures appear in different industries, different markets, different continents. The language changed, the products changed, the leadership styles changed, but the underlying structural failures did not.

Systemisation.
Staffability.
Scalability.
Sustainability.
Sellability.

These five truths followed me everywhere I went.

I first began shaping them in the late 1990s, long before frameworks became fashionable. They weren't theory, they were survival. Every time a company stumbled, at least one of the five pillars had weakened. Every time a company surged, all five were aligned. It became so predictable that eventually, I could walk into a boardroom and sense which pillar was carrying more weight than it should, and which one was beginning to drift.

For years, the Five Pillars formed the backbone of my work with FTSE 100 and Fortune 500 leaders. They allowed me to diagnose fast, intervene precisely, and strengthen organisations in ways that lasted longer than enthusiasm ever could. But even with their power, something felt incomplete.

The structure was clear, but the source of the structure was not.

It took dozens of engagements, and the humility to admit something was missing, before I realised the truth:
Architecture alone cannot explain why a company behaves the way it does. Before structure, there must be identity.

So in 2001, more than two decades ago, I introduced what eventually became 3XV™ into the methodology. Not as a trendy model, not as a theoretical exercise, but as the compass that made the Five Pillars finally make sense.

Vision shapes direction.
Value shapes relevance.

11

Vehicle shapes scalability.

The Five Pillars are the architecture.
3XV™ is the engine that powers it.

Without the engine, the structure is empty.
Without the structure, the engine is dangerous.

This book exists to give you both.

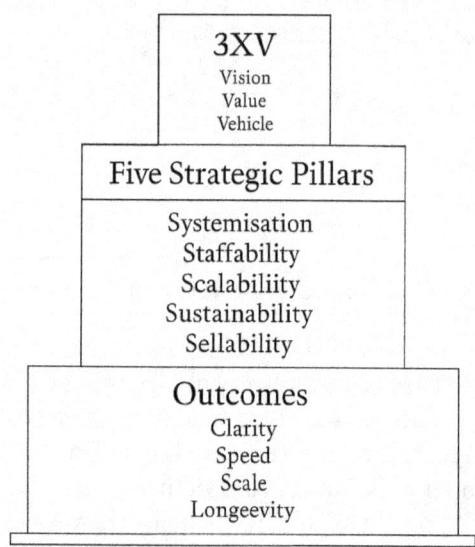

An Invitation Into Structural Clarity

If you have made it this far, allow me to offer the same invitation I extend to the leaders I mentor:
for the next few hours, suspend the belief that effort, talent, or even strategy alone determine your organisation's future. They influence it, yes, but they do not define it. Architecture does.

This book is not written to entertain you, or to motivate you, or to give you comforting ideas you can nod along to and forget. It is written to challenge you, gently, quietly, but firmly. It will interrupt assumptions you've carried for years. It will make you question decisions you once believed were sound. It will ask more of your honesty than your energy.

Because clarity has a cost.
And every great leader eventually pays it.

In the chapters ahead, you will see your organisation through an architectural lens, a way of thinking that reveals what effort has been hiding, what culture has been absorbing, and what success has masked. You will learn why companies drift without noticing, why growth becomes a trap for the unprepared, and why the most dangerous fractures are the ones leaders feel but cannot yet see.

If you let the questions in this book do their work, you will never look at your organisation the same way again.
You will begin to sense weight before it becomes strain.
You will feel drift before it becomes failure.
You will recognise misalignment before it becomes cost.

Most importantly, you will learn to rebuild from truth, not hope.

This is not a textbook.
It is a structural companion for the next decade of your leadership, a way to design a company capable of scaling without breaking, sustaining without exhausting, and succeeding without losing itself.

The invitation is simple:
Step into clarity.
Let architecture show you what movement cannot.
And as we enter Chapter 1, walk with me into the moment I first realised that effort alone is not enough.

CHAPTER 1:
The Day I Realised Architecture Beats Effort

A Boardroom Full of Brilliant People and a Fracture They Could Not See

I still remember the morning it happened, the morning I realised, with absolute clarity, that effort means nothing when architecture is wrong. The moment lives in my memory not because of drama or confrontation, but because of how quietly the truth revealed itself.

I had been invited to sit with a leadership team whose reputation stretched far beyond their industry. They were known for their intelligence, their discipline, their execution. They were the kind of team other companies studied, admired, and envied. Brilliant people, genuinely brilliant, not just in education or experience, but in their ability to think, to adapt, to lead.

Which is why what I saw that day surprised me.

The boardroom itself was immaculate, glass walls, polished surfaces, London skyline stretching behind us. Everything looked intentional, as if the room had been designed to reflect the precision of the company it housed. I took my seat, expecting a strong, focused discussion on the future.

But the atmosphere told a different story.

Leaders often assume that tension announces itself loudly. It doesn't. It appears in subtleties, the kind that experience teaches you to trust long before you can articulate. That morning, the subtleties were everywhere. A stiffness in posture. Eyes that lingered too long on the table. Smiles that didn't reach the eyes. The slight hesitation when someone spoke, as if choosing words that wouldn't provoke discomfort.

These were exceptional leaders, yet they looked unsettled without knowing why.

The CEO began the meeting with updates. Revenue was strong. Margins were holding. Market share had increased. Their new initiative was gaining traction. Everything on paper looked clean, sharp, upward. A story of success.

But I wasn't listening to the numbers.
I was listening to the gaps between them.

When the COO spoke, his presentation was crisp, but his voice carried a strain I recognised instantly, the strain of someone holding pressure he hadn't yet admitted to himself. The CFO spoke next, her tone confident, but her eyes kept glancing sideways, checking the room for something she couldn't find. Even the Head of People, usually the emotional heartbeat of the organisation, seemed unusually guarded.

The fractures were there, invisible to them, unavoidable to me.

About twenty minutes into the meeting, the first real signal appeared. The CEO paused mid-sentence, looked out the window, and exhaled quietly before continuing. That exhale may sound insignificant, but in a high-performance environment, it is a tell. A momentary surrender, the body acknowledging what the mind refuses to voice.

I leaned back slightly, studying the room the way an engineer studies a bridge under load.
The structure was no longer carrying the weight of the organisation's ambition.

It wasn't that the team lacked intelligence or effort. Quite the opposite. They were working harder than ever, longer hours, more meetings, more initiatives, more firefighting disguised as leadership. But effort had become their default response to every challenge, and effort is the most deceptive form of progress. It creates movement without guaranteeing alignment. It creates momentum without ensuring stability.

And when a company accelerates without architecture, something always gives way.

As the conversation continued, patterns emerged. Decisions were being revisited too often. Priorities were shifting weekly. Projects were overlapping without clarity on who owned what. Teams were busy, impressively busy, but not moving in one direction. Success had become noisy, not coherent.

This is what I call the brilliant drift, when talented people compensate for structural weakness with personal effort, masking the truth that the system underneath is beginning to fail.

At one point, the COO shared a slide showing their growth trajectory. It looked impressive, almost enviable. But as he spoke, I watched the CTO subtly shake his head, not in disagreement, but in resignation. He knew something wasn't right. He could feel the strain, but he didn't yet understand its origin.

That was the moment I realised the room was full of brilliant people who were blind to the fracture forming beneath them.

They weren't incompetent. They weren't negligent. They weren't unaware. They were simply too close to see what I could.

It's the curse of leadership, the closer you are to the work, the harder it becomes to see the structure.

Eventually, the CEO turned to me.
"Moe, what are you seeing?" he asked.

I hesitated for a moment, not out of uncertainty, but out of respect. The truth was clear, but truth delivered too early can trigger defensiveness in even the strongest leaders.

What I saw was this:

The organisation was succeeding on the surface, but failing underneath.
Effort was carrying the company, not architecture.
The people were holding the weight, not the pillars.

I looked around the table, at the fatigue hiding behind their professionalism, at the tension masked by polite updates, at the hope that the next initiative would fix what only structural redesign could repair.

"You're not aligned," I finally said, gently. "You're moving fast, but not together. And the speed is exposing the structure."

Silence.

Not discomfort. Not resistance.
Recognition.

They felt it.
They always had.
They just didn't have the language for it.

This was the moment that changed everything for me, and for them. The moment I understood, unequivocally, that effort is finite, but architecture is not. That the smartest teams can still drift. And that brilliance, without structure, eventually breaks under its own weight.

That day, in that room, I realised that the real work of leadership is not keeping people busy.
It is building an organisation designed to carry the future without collapsing.

And that truth became the foundation of everything I teach today.

My First Major Failure as a Young Consultant

You never forget the first time you fail publicly, painfully, and undeniably in front of a leader who trusted you. My first major failure as a young consultant didn't just bruise my confidence, it reshaped the way I would see organisations for the rest of my life.

I was still early in my career, filled with enthusiasm, ambition, and a dangerous belief that effort could solve anything. Back then, I equated long hours with impact, activity with progress, and intelligence with capability. I thought if I worked harder than anyone else in the room, the results would follow.

Looking back now, I realise how naïve that was.

The company was a respected FTSE brand, stable, admired, envied. When they approached me, it felt like a breakthrough moment. I walked into their headquarters feeling accomplished, prepared, and more confident than my experience warranted. The atrium was bright, the halls buzzing with movement, the people sharp and disciplined. Everything about the organisation felt solid.

At least, that's what I thought at the time.

My assignment involved helping them accelerate a core strategic program that the board believed would redefine the company's future. The initiative had visibility, resources, and urgency. I was eager, too eager, to prove myself. I threw myself into the work with intensity. Meetings, workshops, late nights, endless analysis… I mistook activity for effectiveness.

And because I was young, the team admired the energy. I confused admiration for correctness.

The first signs of trouble were subtle, the same kind of subtlety I would learn years later to treat as structural warning signs. A decision delayed here. A team out of sync there. A department drowning quietly under responsibilities no one had acknowledged. I noticed these things, but I didn't know what they meant. I saw friction, but not architecture. I saw symptoms, but not the load-bearing patterns underneath them.

I believed then that friction simply meant people needed more coordination.

More energy.
More clarity.
More effort.

So I pushed harder.

And in pushing harder, I pushed the organisation faster than its structure could support.

The real collapse didn't happen suddenly. It happened in stages, in the quiet erosion that takes place when an organisation accelerates beyond its design. People began burning out. Deadlines began slipping. Meetings multiplied. Decisions froze. What looked like momentum was actually strain, and the more strain appeared, the more effort everyone poured in to compensate.

It was a perfect storm: high talent, high drive, low structural awareness.

I was the one unintentionally fuelling it.

The moment the truth became impossible to ignore arrived in a boardroom that I remember with painful clarity. The senior executive sponsoring the program, a man known for his composure and analytical mind, had always been supportive. He trusted me, defended me, and gave me the freedom to run. I mistook his trust for confirmation that everything was on the right track.

During one of our review meetings, I presented a detailed update. I talked about the energy, the progress, the milestones we were hitting, the alignment I believed we were building. I painted a picture of forward movement.

When I finished, he didn't speak.

He just looked at me, not angrily, not impatiently, but with a level of stillness that made the room feel small.

Then he asked one question:

"Where is the structure that will hold all of this together?"

One question.
Nine words.
And everything inside me collapsed.

Because I didn't have an answer.

Not a real one.
Not an architectural one.

I had activity, enthusiasm, and effort, but no structure. I had movement without integrity. Momentum without stability. A plan without a load-bearing foundation. I had been so focused on pushing the work forward that I had never stopped to ask whether the organisation beneath it was capable of carrying the weight.

He exhaled, not in frustration but in disappointment, a disappointment I had earned.

"Moe," he said quietly, "you've worked incredibly hard. But you've worked on the wrong thing."

Those words cut deeper than any criticism I've ever received.
Not because they were harsh, but because they were true.

I had failed him.
I had failed the organisation.
And worst of all, I had failed to see the fracture forming beneath what I thought was progress.

In the weeks that followed, the initiative unraveled. People were exhausted. Costs ballooned. Internal trust weakened. The program stalled. I could feel the disappointment in every room I walked into, even when no one said it explicitly.

Failure teaches in ways success never can.

That moment forced me to confront a truth that would become foundational in my work:

Effort is a poor substitute for architecture.

It doesn't matter how talented the people are, how motivated the teams are, or how ambitious the leaders are. If the structure cannot hold the direction, the organisation will eventually collapse, quietly at first, then loudly.

That failure reshaped me.

It humbled me.
It slowed me down.
It sharpened my instincts.
It made me question what I thought I understood.
It pushed me to look beneath the surface of every organisation I entered.

It also taught me a truth I carry into every boardroom to this day:

A leader can be brilliant, a company can be successful, and a team can be exceptional, and still be one unexamined fracture away from collapse.

That early failure did not break me.
It built me.

It taught me to listen to the room, not the slides.
To follow the pressure, not the narrative.
To trust what architecture reveals long before the data confirms it.

And that lesson, painful, precise, unforgettable, is the reason I became the Strategic Architect leaders call today.

The Price of Effort Without Architecture

There is a moment in every leader's journey when they realise that effort, no matter how noble, disciplined, or relentless, eventually extracts a price. I learned that price far earlier than I wanted to, and far later than I should have. It took the collapse of that FTSE initiative, the disappointment in a senior leader's eyes, and the quiet aftermath of my own misjudgment to understand the real cost of driving a company faster than its architecture can carry.

In the days following my failure, I tried to make sense of what had happened. I replayed decisions, conversations, milestones, and meetings the way you replay a car accident in your mind, trying to identify the exact moment when everything slipped out of your control. The truth, of course, was more subtle. There wasn't a single moment. There were dozens, small, quiet warnings I ignored because I believed effort would compensate.

This is how effort blinds leaders:
It convinces them that movement equals progress.
It convinces them that momentum equals strength.
It convinces them that hard work can overcome structural drift.

But the more I examined the situation, the clearer it became: our problem had nothing to do with commitment or competence. Everyone involved worked hard. Everyone cared. Everyone tried. Effort was not the missing ingredient. Architecture was.

Without structure, effort becomes strain.
Without clarity, effort becomes conflict.
Without design, effort becomes waste.
Without alignment, effort becomes exhaustion.

And exhaustion is always the bill that effort eventually sends.

I saw it in the faces of the teams, the quiet fatigue that leaders misinterpret as lack of motivation. I saw it in the repeated meetings that solved nothing because decisions had nowhere to anchor. I saw it in duplicated work, confused priorities, and projects that looked promising but never gained traction. The organisation was drowning, not because people weren't working, but because their work had no structural container to hold it.

It was like pouring water into a cracked vase.
The harder you try, the faster it leaks.

As the weeks went by, I became painfully aware of something I had missed entirely: effort, when misapplied, becomes oppressive. Not intentionally, not maliciously, but structurally. When an organisation has no architectural clarity, every person is forced to work harder just to stand still. Leaders compensate with intensity. Teams compensate with loyalty. Individuals compensate with late nights. Departments compensate with firefighting disguised as urgency.

But the structure compensates for nothing.

It breaks.

The emotional price of that failure hit me hardest the day the sponsoring executive called me into his office. He didn't raise his voice. He didn't criticise. He spoke slowly, almost gently, in a way that made the truth harder to hear.

"Moe," he said, "your heart is in the right place. But effort is not strategy. And strategy is not structure."

At the time, those words felt like a rebuke.
Now, I understand them as a gift.

Because what he was really telling me was this:

If the architecture is wrong, effort will betray you.

You can push harder, but the friction increases.
You can grow faster, but the cracks widen.
You can motivate people, but the fatigue deepens.
You can celebrate wins, but the drift continues.

What I realised, painfully, but with clarity, is that leaders often overestimate what effort can achieve and underestimate what architecture prevents. Effort can create movement, but it cannot create coherence. Effort can deliver tasks, but it cannot deliver transformation. Effort can build momentum, but it cannot hold weight.

The price I paid for that misunderstanding wasn't financial. It was human. I watched capable people struggle unnecessarily. I watched departments turn against one another because the structure didn't clarify ownership. I watched a team that was once confident begin to lose faith in its direction. And I watched a leader absorb blame for a failure that was structural, not personal.

That was the day I vowed never to let effort masquerade as architecture again.

I began studying organisations not as collections of people, but as systems carrying weight. Not as departments, but as load-bearing structures. Not as

23

teams, but as interconnected flows. I learned to ask questions I had never considered:

Where is the pressure accumulating?
Where is clarity dissolving?
Where is the decision load too heavy?
Where is the structure misaligned with the ambition?
Where is the system forcing effort to compensate for design flaws?

These questions became my compass.

In the years that followed, I discovered something remarkable: when architecture is right, effort decreases. People work less but achieve more. Decisions accelerate. Meetings shrink. Priorities sharpen. Growth becomes natural, not forced. The organisation stops feeling heavy and begins to feel inevitable.

Leaders often tell me they want a "high-performance culture."
I tell them performance is not created, it's released.
And it's released only when the architecture removes the need for unnecessary effort.

That lesson began with my failure.
It became a lens through which I now see every company I enter.

Effort is admirable.
Effort is honourable.
Effort is necessary.

But effort is not the foundation.
Architecture is.

And until leaders understand that, they will continue paying the price I once paid, a price far higher than they ever intended to spend.

What This Book Will Help You Finally See

If there is one truth I want you to carry from this chapter into every chapter that follows, it is this: most organisations do not collapse because of a single catastrophic event. They collapse because of a thousand quiet moments where nobody noticed the architecture drifting.

That is what this book will help you finally see.

Most leaders are trained to look at performance. They track metrics, analyse dashboards, review targets, optimise processes, and measure output. All of this is useful, but none of it reveals the underlying structure. Performance tells you what happened. Architecture tells you why it happened, and what will happen next.

What this book will show you is how to see your organisation the way an architect sees a building: not by its façade, but by its load-bearing design.

You will begin to recognise the difference between effort and integrity, the difference between a company that survives because its people are compensating, and a company that thrives because its structure is carrying the weight. You will start to sense drift long before it becomes visible. You will notice hesitations in meetings not as behavioural quirks, but as structural signals. You will learn to hear the truth behind the silence.

You will also learn why brilliant teams break, even when their leaders are intelligent, capable, and committed. It is rarely because of incompetence. It is almost always because the architecture they inherited can no longer support the ambition they carry. This book will give you the language to describe what your instincts have been telling you for years, that something feels "off," even when no one can point to a specific failure.

This book will help you see the invisible fracture.

The fracture is not dramatic. It rarely shows up in the financials until it is too late. Instead, it appears in patterns: decisions that slow down, meetings that multiply, communication that becomes vague, priorities that shift without explanation. These are not operational issues. They are architectural warnings. And once you learn to recognise them, you will never look at your organisation the same way again.

You will see why companies with extraordinary talent still struggle to scale. You will understand why teams become exhausted even when workloads seem reasonable. You will learn why strategies fail despite being logically sound. You will discover why the systems you've built sometimes fight against you instead of supporting you.

And most importantly, you will understand that the answers are not found in working harder, but in designing smarter.

This book is not here to motivate you. It is not here to convince you that you need to be more, do more, or push more. You already push enough. What you need, what most leaders desperately need, is clarity. Structural clarity. Architectural clarity. Clarity that cuts through the noise, reveals the truth, and gives you the confidence to rebuild, reshape, and refine.

You will see how the Five Strategic Pillars, Systemisation, Staffability, Scalability, Sustainability, and Sellability, act as the organisational spine. You will understand why these Pillars collapse when misaligned, and why they become unstoppable when powered by 3XV™, the strategic identity engine that sits above them.

You will begin to see why I have spent decades refining this methodology, why leaders call me at their most vulnerable moments, and why some ask me to sign agreements preventing me from helping their competitors. It is not because I bring magic. It is because I bring sight. The ability to see what they cannot, or what they can feel but cannot explain.

If you let it, this book will give you that same sight.

It will help you understand the difference between fixing symptoms and redesigning structure. It will help you recognise the patterns that lead to drift. It will show you why some companies scale elegantly while others fight their own weight. It will teach you how to read the room, how to sense the fracture, and how to build an organisation capable of carrying your ambition without breaking.

You will see what I saw that day in the boardroom, not the brilliance of the people, but the weakness of the structure. Not the movement, but the misalignment. Not the effort, but the cost of effort. And once you see it, you cannot unsee it.

That is the gift and the burden of architectural awareness.

By the time you finish this book, you will understand why architecture beats effort, every single time.
You will understand why companies drift, why they break, and why they can be rebuilt stronger than before.
You will understand the truth that took me decades to accept: effort is finite, but architecture is infinite.

And as we step into Chapter 2, we will begin with the engine that powers everything, the identity that shapes direction, relevance, and scalability.

We begin with Vision.
Not as an idea, but as architecture.

CHAPTER 2:
The 3XV Strategic Engine™

Vision: Designing the Destination

Most leaders believe they have a vision.
They can describe their goals, their aspirations, their next targets. Some can even articulate a three-year plan, a five-year ambition, or a bold strategic direction. But a real vision, the kind that acts as the architectural blueprint for an organisation, is something far more precise, far more demanding, and far more personal than most leaders ever confront.

A true vision is not a statement.
It's not a paragraph in a deck.
It's not a slogan crafted during a strategy retreat.

A true vision is a decision about the future you are willing to architect, and the future you are willing to reject.

The first time I fully understood this was not during a workshop or strategy session, but during a quiet moment of failure, one of those moments when the world feels brutally honest. It was years ago, long before I created 3XV™, long before the Five Pillars were formalised. I had spent months working with a leadership team who had all the talent, all the resources, and all the market opportunity required for greatness. Yet everything they attempted felt scattered, inconsistent, and heavy.

Their problem wasn't intelligence.
It wasn't capability.
It wasn't even alignment.

Their problem was that they had no destination.
Only movement.

Movement without direction is drift disguised as progress.

When I asked the CEO to define the future he wanted to build, he paused, looked away, and finally admitted something most leaders never say aloud:

"I'm not entirely sure."

That moment stayed with me, because I realised how common, and how costly, that uncertainty truly is. Leaders rarely admit that their vision is vague, but their organisations feel it. When the destination is blurry, everything underneath begins to wobble. Decisions lose coherence. Priorities shift weekly. Teams start guessing. Momentum becomes noise.

Vision is the first of the 3XV™ elements because without it, nothing else can hold. Not systems. Not people. Not scale. Not sustainability. Vision is the load-bearing beam that determines the entire structural path of the organisation.

Vision is not what you want. It is what the organisation must become.

This distinction matters.

Leaders often approach vision as a personal wish list: growth, expansion, market dominance, new products, new geographies. But those are outcomes, not architecture. Vision must answer a more structural question:

What future configuration of the organisation will make the next decade inevitable instead of accidental?

That question forced me, years ago, to confront a painful truth about my own career: I had been helping companies move faster without always ensuring they were moving toward something structurally sound. I had mistaken ambition for vision, and forward motion for direction. It took several missteps, including the early failures I described in Chapter 1, for me to understand that designing the destination is the real work of leadership.

Vision is clarity.

Clarity is structure.
Structure is destiny.

Over the years, I've sat with hundreds of leaders who believed they had a clear vision. But as we unpacked it, the clarity dissolved. Here are the three patterns I see most often:

1. **The Expansive Vision**
   A long list of ambitions that sound impressive but lack definition. The organisation becomes diluted, overstretched, confused.

2. **The Reactive Vision**

A future shaped by competitors, trends, or fear. The organisation becomes defensive, operationally heavy, and emotionally exhausted.

3. **The Comfortable Vision**
   A future that resembles the present, only bigger. The organisation stagnates, unable to break the gravity of its own history.

None of these are visions. They are coping mechanisms.

A real vision has sharp edges. It has weight. It narrows the path, not widens it. It excludes more than it includes. Leaders often resist this because exclusion feels limiting, but structurally, exclusion creates integrity.

Architecture requires boundaries.
Without boundaries, you do not have a design, you have a wishlist.

The moment Vision becomes real

A vision becomes real at the exact moment it answers five architectural questions:

- *What future are we architecting toward?*

- *What future are we deliberately walking away from?*

- *What does the organisation need to become structurally in order to carry that future?*

- *What load-bearing elements must be strengthened for that future to hold?*

- *What beliefs must the leadership team outgrow to get there?*

The last question is the hardest.
Most organisations do not fail because of external forces.
They fail because leaders outgrow their markets faster than they outgrow themselves.

Vision demands self-confrontation

I remember working with a founder who had grown his company from a kitchen table to £86M. He was brilliant, creative, driven, sharp. But his vision was anchored in who he had been, not who he needed to become. His organisation had reached a point where founder-driven decision-making was restricting scale. Yet every time we attempted to define a future where his role shifted, he pulled back.

Not because he couldn't imagine it.
But because he didn't know who he would be without the chaos he had mastered.

Vision forces leaders to answer a question they often avoid:

Can you design a future that no longer needs the version of you that built the past?

If not, the organisation remains trapped in its previous architecture.

Vision shapes the Pillars

What leaders often miss is that the Five Strategic Pillars are not neutral. They bend around the Vision. For example:

- A Vision built on high-touch service requires Systemisation that protects intimacy, not just efficiency.

- A Vision built on rapid scale requires Staffability that redesigns leadership load, not just headcount.

- A Vision built on global expansion requires Sustainability practices that anticipate timezone complexity, cultural drift, and strategic fatigue.

- A Vision built on eventual exit requires Sellability that embeds independence from the founders years before it is needed.

Without Vision, the Pillars work against each other.
With Vision, they form an integrated spine.

32

Why leaders resist true Vision

Many leaders avoid defining a destination for one simple reason:

Once you define it, you become accountable to it.

Ambiguity gives leaders emotional comfort.
Clarity gives them responsibility.

A leader once told me, "If I declare the future, I can no longer hide behind the present."
He was right.

Vision removes the excuses.
Vision removes the noise.
Vision removes the comfortable wiggle room.

Because vision is not an aspiration.
It is a structural commitment.

The day I learned the weight of Vision

There was a moment, early in my transition from consultant to Strategic Architect, when I realised how much damage unclear vision creates. I was advising a company preparing for aggressive expansion. They were talented, well-funded, respected. But every part of the organisation was pulling in a slightly different direction. Teams were making logical decisions, but not aligned ones. The CEO kept adjusting the strategy because he had not yet decided the future he was actually building toward.

I finally said to him:
"Your organisation isn't confused. It's following you."

He stared at me in silence.
Then he whispered, "I haven't declared the destination, have I?"

He hadn't.
And as soon as he did, the entire company shifted.

People became sharper.
Decisions became faster.
Conflicts decreased.
Systems aligned.
Culture stabilised.

Not because anything new was added, but because ambiguity was removed.

Vision is the first design decision

Everything in your company, every process, every hire, every cost, every conflict, every priority, either supports the Vision or erodes it.
There is no neutral state.

The question is not whether you have a Vision.
The question is whether the one you have is architected, or accidental.

The purpose of this chapter

Vision is the first of the 3XV elements because nothing structural can hold without it.
In the chapters ahead:

- Value will define why the market chooses you.

- Vehicle will define how your business model carries your promise.

But Vision comes first because it answers the defining question:

Where are we going, and who must we become to get there?

When leaders finally confront that question with honesty, the architecture begins to shift.
The organisation begins to breathe.
The future becomes more than a hope, it becomes a design.

And design is the beginning of all transformation.

Value: Why the Market Chooses You or Leaves You

If Vision determines the destination, Value determines whether anyone will walk with you.

Value is often treated as a marketing exercise, a message, a USP, a positioning statement. Leaders talk about "communicating value," "packaging value," "adding value," as if value is something they hand to the market like a gift.

But value is not something you declare.
Value is something the market decides.

The market is the judge, not the audience. It doesn't care how hard you work, how passionate your team is, or how much potential you believe you have. The market responds to one thing:

The perceived value of your contribution compared to the alternative.

When I first understood this, truly understood it, it shifted the way I viewed business forever.

It wasn't during a high-profile engagement.
It wasn't in a FTSE boardroom.
It was during a moment of quiet humiliation early in my career.

A client, one I was deeply invested in, abruptly shifted their budget away from the strategy we had spent weeks designing. They chose a competitor instead. Not because he had a better solution. Not because he had better credentials. But because, in their eyes, he offered higher value in that moment. I had assumed my effort guaranteed my relevance. The market proved otherwise.

That day taught me a truth that leaders often resist:

You are not chosen because you are good. You are chosen because you are valuable.
And value is measured in outcomes, not effort.

The Illusion of Value

Most leaders overestimate the value they deliver and underestimate the value the market expects. This gap, between perceived value and required value, is where companies lose relevance, customers, and eventually their position.

I see three recurring illusions:

1. The Competence Illusion

Leaders believe being technically good is enough.
 It isn't.

The market doesn't reward competence.
It assumes competence.
It rewards transformation.

2. The Effort Illusion

Leaders assume that because they work hard, the market will stay loyal.
It won't.

Effort creates internal pride.
Value creates external demand.

3. The Legacy Illusion

Leaders assume that because they were valuable in the past, they will continue to be valuable in the future.
They won't, unless they continuously re-architect that value.

Markets evolve.
Competitors adapt.
Customer expectations shift.
Technology rewrites the rules.

Your value must move faster than your history.

Value Is Not What You Think It Is

I once met a founder who confidently declared,
"Our value is quality."

I asked him, "According to whom?"

He paused. He had assumed the market agreed because he believed it. But
in the market's eyes, the value wasn't quality, it was convenience. His
competitors weren't winning because they had better products. They were
winning because they made life easier for the customer.

Value, I told him, is not the thing you admire about yourself.
Value is the thing the customer cannot live without.

Over the years, I've noticed something fascinating:
Companies collapse not because they stop delivering value,
but because they deliver value no one cares about anymore.

What was once meaningful becomes irrelevant.
What was once impressive becomes expected.
What was once unique becomes common.

Value must be re-architected, not defended.

How Value Shapes the Architecture

When leaders misunderstand Value, they build the wrong architecture.
They design systems, teams, and models around what they *want* to deliver
instead of what the market is willing to pay for.

Here's the structural truth:
Every part of your organisation exists to deliver value, nothing else.

Your systems exist to deliver value consistently.
Your people exist to deliver value collaboratively.
Your growth engine exists to deliver value at scale.
Your sustainability practices exist to deliver value predictably.
Your sellability depends on whether that value is transferable.

When Value is misunderstood, all Five Pillars become misaligned
simultaneously.

It is the most dangerous misalignment of all, because it feels like progress
until the market reveals otherwise.

The Day a FTSE Leader Taught Me What Value Really Means

Years ago, I was working with a FTSE company preparing to acquire a smaller competitor. The financials made sense. The strategic logic was strong. But something felt off.

During a meeting, the acquiring CEO asked a question that froze the room:

"Does the market actually want what they're selling,
 or are we projecting our own value onto them?"

Silence.

It was a profound question, because it exposed a structural blind spot: the assumption that customers value what we value. They don't. They value the outcome they experience, not the product you admire.

We ran a rapid analysis. What we discovered was shocking: while the target company was deeply proud of its technical superiority, customers were leaving because they felt overwhelmed by complexity. The company's greatest pride was the market's greatest frustration.

They weren't losing because they were weak.
They were losing because their value was misaligned.

That acquisition never happened.
It saved the FTSE company millions.

More importantly, it taught me something I've never forgotten:

Value is only valuable when the market agrees.

The Emotional Side of Value

Leaders rarely talk about the emotional cost of losing relevance.
It feels personal, because it is.

When the market stops choosing you, it doesn't just hurt financially.
It hurts your identity, your confidence, your belief in your own competence.
It shakes your certainty.

I've watched brilliant leaders crumble under the weight of value erosion.
Not because they lacked skills, but because they clung to a version of value
the market had outgrown.

The most successful leaders I've worked with share one trait:
They redesign their value before the market forces them to.

That requires humility.
It requires discipline.
And it requires understanding the architecture of value.

The Architecture of Value: Three Load-Bearing Questions

Whenever I work with a company, I ask three questions that reveal
everything:

1. What does the market believe your value is?

Not what **you** believe, what **they** believe.

2. What future value is the market already drifting toward?

The next three years matter more than the last ten.

3. What must your organisation become structurally to deliver that value effortlessly?

If delivering value requires heroics, you don't have value, you have strain.

These questions uncover fractures leaders never see.

For some, the fracture is in the model.
For others, it's in the experience.
For many, it's in the assumption that value is permanent.

Why Value Determines Whether You Scale or Stall

No company scales because of its ambition.
Companies scale because their value is:

- **Clear**

- **Compelling**

- **Consistent**

- **Commercially validated**

If value is unclear, growth becomes heavy.
If value is unremarkable, growth becomes slow.
If value is inconsistent, growth becomes unpredictable.
If value is outdated, growth becomes impossible.

I've witnessed eight-figure companies hit ceilings not because they lacked opportunity, but because their value had not evolved. They were trying to scale a version of themselves the market no longer wanted.

Value is the oxygen of scale.
When it weakens, everything suffocates.

What This Book Will Help You Understand About Value

By the end of this chapter, you will understand three truths:

1. Value is architectural, not emotional.

It determines structure, systems, staffing, and strategy.

2. Value must be re-earned, not assumed.

Past value is history.
Future value is design.

3. Value is the deciding factor in whether the Pillars strengthen or collapse.

A strong Vision sets the destination.
But Value decides whether the world walks with you.

Where We Go Next

Now that you understand why Vision determines direction and Value establishes relevance, we move to the third, and often most misunderstood, part of the 3XV engine:

Vehicle: the engine that carries your promise.

Most companies don't fail because of their Vision.
They fail because they chose the wrong Vehicle.

And that is where we go next.

Vehicle: The Engine That Carries Your Promise

If Vision sets the destination, and Value determines whether the market chooses you, then the Vehicle is the engine, the structural choice, that determines whether your organisation can actually get there.

In my early years, I underestimated how critical this choice was. I believed that if the vision was clear and the value compelling, the model would naturally fall into place. But time and experience have taught me something different, something far more unforgiving:

A brilliant vision riding in the wrong vehicle never arrives.
A powerful value proposition carried by the wrong model collapses under its own weight.

Leaders rarely realise this until it's too late.

The Misalignment That Nearly Broke a Great Company

One of my earliest and most sobering lessons came from a fast-growing firm that was admired across its industry. They had vision, a bold, precise, ambitious future. They had value, the market loved what they offered. And they had talent, some of the best people I've ever worked with.

But they were trapped in the wrong vehicle.

Their business model was built for depth, yet their ambition demanded scale. Their infrastructure was designed for craftsmanship, yet their market was shifting toward speed. The very vehicle that had made them successful was now the same vehicle making success impossible to sustain.

As they accelerated, the model resisted.
As they added staff, margins shrank.
As they added clients, operations buckled.
As they pushed harder, the structure pushed back.

They believed they had a performance problem.
What they had was a Vehicle problem.

It was the first time I saw something I would later witness in dozens of companies:

When the Vehicle is wrong, every effort becomes friction.
When the Vehicle is right, effort becomes momentum.

The Vehicle Is Not Your Product.

It's Not Your Service.
It's Not Your Price.

The Vehicle is the structural design of how value flows to the customer and revenue flows back to the business.

Business-to-business.
Business-to-consumer.
Subscription.
One-off sales.
Licensing.
Platform.
Marketplace.
Enterprise.
Franchising.
Hybrid.
Agency.
Productised service.
Self-serve.
High-touch.
Low-touch.
AI-enabled.
Human-led.
Orchestration.
Automation.

These are not labels.
They are architectures.

Each has different load paths, different stress points, different scaling limitations, different staffing implications, and different capital requirements. A Vehicle is not chosen for convenience. It is chosen for alignment.

When leaders pick a Vehicle that contradicts their Vision or cannot sustain their Value, the organisation is doomed to fight itself.

Why Leaders Choose the Wrong Vehicle

I've seen three recurring causes:

1. Legacy Attachment

Leaders cling to the model that made them successful. They forget that success is historical, not predictive. The model that carried them for the first decade may be the very model that prevents the next decade.

2. Emotional Preference

Some leaders choose a Vehicle because they like how it feels. They enjoy certain types of work, or certain types of clients, or certain ways of operating. They confuse personal preference with structural necessity.

3. Market Illusion

Leaders copy competitors who appear successful, assuming the same model will work for them. But a Vehicle is contextual. What works for one organisation may destroy another.

The most dangerous phrase I hear in boardrooms is:
"This is how we've always done it."

The second most dangerous is:
"This model works for them, it should work for us."

Vehicles are not transferable.
They are architectural commitments.

The Day I Chose the Wrong Vehicle Myself

It would be easy to pretend that this clarity came without cost.
It didn't.

Years ago, I attempted to build a small consulting offer in a delivery model that fundamentally contradicted my own philosophy. At the time, it seemed viable. Quick to set up. Easy to package. Easy for clients to say yes to.

But the model demanded a pace and style of delivery that stripped away depth, and depth is the oxygen of my work.

Clients were satisfied.
But I wasn't.
And more importantly, they weren't receiving the transformation they deserved.

The model was misaligned with the promise.
The Vehicle didn't match the value.

And so I killed it.

That experience taught me a painful but necessary truth:
A misaligned Vehicle doesn't just weaken the business, it weakens the leader.

It makes you feel like you're delivering with one hand tied behind your back. It forces you to compromise the experience, the results, or the integrity of the work.

When the Vehicle is wrong, even excellence becomes exhausting.

The Vehicle Determines Scalability

Many companies believe they have a scale problem.
In reality, they have a Vehicle problem.

Consider this architectural truth:

A Vehicle built for craft cannot scale for volume.

A Vehicle built for volume cannot sustain craft.

A high-touch model cannot survive in a margin-sensitive market.
A low-touch model cannot survive in a market that requires intimacy.
A subscription model collapses if value is episodic instead of continuous.
A one-off service model collapses if value is cumulative instead of immediate.

Most eight-figure companies that stall do not stall because of leadership failure.
They stall because the Vehicle they chose at £3M cannot carry them to £30M.

Their systems can scale.
Their people can scale.
Their clients can scale.
Even their value can scale.

But their Vehicle cannot.

No amount of effort will change that.
Only redesign will.

The Vehicle Determines Talent

Staffability, the second Pillar, is shaped heavily by the Vehicle.

A professional services model requires decision-makers, not doers.
A product model requires engineers and support.
A subscription model requires retention architecture.
A licensing model requires compliance.
A platform model requires ecosystem thinking.
A marketplace model requires dual-sided trust orchestration.

When the Vehicle is wrong, leaders hire the wrong people, reward the wrong behaviours, and organise teams around the wrong truths.

I've seen brilliant people fail in the wrong models and ordinary people thrive in the right ones. The difference was never the people. It was always the architecture they were placed inside.

The Vehicle Determines Culture

Culture is not built from values on a wall.
It emerges from structural realities.

A high-volume model creates urgency.
A low-volume model creates depth.
A franchise model creates control.
A creative model creates freedom.
A recurring-revenue model creates stability.
A transactional model creates pressure.

Your Vehicle teaches your people how to behave.
It shapes leadership cadence.
It shapes communication.
It shapes emotion.
It shapes expectation.

Culture is architecture wearing a human face.

The Vehicle Determines What Breaks First

Every Vehicle has a predictable point of failure:

- Services break at utilisation.

- Product companies break at iteration speed.

- Subscription models break at churn.

- Agencies break at leadership bandwidth.

- Platforms break at adoption.

- Marketplaces break at imbalance.

- Enterprise models break at sales cycles.

- Creator-led businesses break at founder dependency.

When leaders understand their Vehicle deeply, they can diagnose drift early.
When they don't, breakdown feels sudden, but it never is.

The Vehicle Determines Sellability

One of the greatest misconceptions in entrepreneurship is that sellability is about financials.
It isn't.

Buyers care about the Vehicle.

A misaligned Vehicle requires too much effort from the next owner.
A fragile Vehicle requires too much risk.
A founder-dependent Vehicle cannot be transferred.
A complexity-heavy Vehicle cannot be scaled.

The market doesn't buy businesses.
It buys architectures.

How You Know the Vehicle Is Wrong

There are seven emotional signals:

- The business feels heavier every year.

- Growth requires more effort, not more clarity.

- Decisions take longer.

- You have more meetings but fewer outcomes.

- People look busy but traction feels slow.

- You are constantly "fixing" instead of redesigning.

- Success feels fragile instead of inevitable.

These are not operational issues.
They are architectural warnings.

What the Right Vehicle Feels Like

Leaders often ask,
"How will I know when we've chosen the right one?"

You'll know because the organisation exhale.

Work becomes clean.
Teams become sharper.
Systems begin to reinforce each other.
Culture regains rhythm.
Leadership workload decreases.
Clients feel the difference.
The organisation feels like it is finally moving *with* itself.

The right Vehicle doesn't just carry the promise,
it amplifies it.

Where This Takes Us Next

With Vision defined, Value clarified, and Vehicle understood as the architectural engine beneath everything, we now reach the structural turning point of this book.

In the next section, we explore the truth most leaders avoid:

When 3XV is wrong, nothing else works.
Not the Pillars.
Not the systems.
Not the people.
Not the growth.

When 3XV Is Wrong, Nothing Else Works

There is a moment in every major advisory engagement when the truth reveals itself, unmistakably and brutally: the organisation is not breaking because of its people, or its systems, or its market. It is breaking because the strategic identity, the very core of 3XV™, is misaligned.

When Vision is unclear, Value outdated, or Vehicle wrong, the entire organisation becomes confused, heavy, and structurally unstable. The Pillars buckle. Teams become exhausted. Leaders become reactive. Culture becomes brittle. And the organisation begins compensating with effort, hoping that movement will mask the drift.

It never does.

This was one of the most difficult truths for me to accept early in my career, because so often the symptoms appeared elsewhere. People pointed to systems, staff issues, market conditions, or execution failures. Leaders blamed motivation, accountability, or communication breakdowns. But beneath all of it, beneath every collapse I have ever witnessed, sat the same foundational truth:

Identity determines architecture.
Architecture determines performance.
Performance determines results.

And when identity is wrong, nothing underneath it can hold.

The FTSE Company That Looked Perfect — And Was Drifting Quietly

Years ago, I worked with a FTSE company admired across its sector. Their numbers were strong. Their leadership team was brilliant. Their market position enviable. But something subtle was shifting, a kind of organisational fatigue that had no visible cause.

Teams were working harder than ever.
Systems were being refined.
Processes were redesigned.
Leadership initiatives were launched.

Yet the organisation was slipping.

At first glance, it looked like a Staffability issue, the people were overwhelmed. Then it appeared like a Systemisation failure, too many handoffs, too many bottlenecks. Then it looked like a Scalability constraint, the company was growing faster than its infrastructure.

But all of those were symptoms.
 The fracture was above the Pillars.

The real issue was Vision drift.
The leadership team had changed the destination without recalibrating the architecture. The company was structurally designed for the future they had outgrown, but not for the future they were now chasing.

The identity was outdated.
The architecture was misaligned.
The behaviour was inconsistent.
And the results were predictable.

This is the pattern I have seen more times than I can count:
When 3XV is wrong, the organisation becomes heavier each year, no matter how hard people work.

Misaligned Vision: When the Destination Doesn't Match the Design

A misaligned Vision creates organisational schizophrenia.
Teams execute today's tasks while unknowingly sabotaging tomorrow's ambitions. The CEO speaks about scaling globally, while the Pillars remain designed for local operations. Leaders speak about innovation, while their culture is structured for risk minimisation. They speak about customer intimacy, while their systems incentivise speed over depth.

When Vision shifts and architecture doesn't, the company drifts into internal contradiction.
Nothing works smoothly.

You cannot build a skyscraper on the blueprint of a bungalow.
Yet leaders try, and pay the price.

Misaligned Value: When the Market Has Moved On

One of the most painful failures to witness is when a company's value proposition is no longer relevant, but the leadership team continues defending it.

The market evolves.
Customers expect different outcomes.
Competitors redefine the standards.
Technology shifts the psychology of buying.
AI reshapes expectations of speed, quality, and personalisation.

But inside the organisation, decisions are still being made based on historic value, the value that once made them great, but no longer makes them chosen.

Nothing breaks a leader faster than discovering their value has expired.

The company tries to compensate through marketing, pricing, and performance pressure, but when Value is wrong, nothing else works.

Systems buckle because they're built to deliver value no one wants.
Staffability breaks because people are rewarded for the wrong things.
Scalability becomes impossible because you cannot scale irrelevance.
Sustainability collapses because the business model fights the market.
Sellability disappears because no buyer wants a company attached to a fading value proposition.

Value is oxygen.
When it goes stale, the company suffocates.

Misaligned Vehicle: When the Engine Cannot Carry the Promise

Vision may be inspiring.
Value may be compelling.
But if the Vehicle, the business model, cannot carry the promise, everything becomes heavy.

A premium value proposition inside a low-margin model always collapses.
A speed-driven value proposition inside a craftsmanship model becomes chaotic.
A global vision inside a founder-dependent model is impossible.
A recurring revenue promise inside a high-variability model destroys profitability.

This is where most eight-figure companies fail.
They believe they have execution issues.
They actually have Vehicle misalignment.

When the Vehicle is wrong, people work harder but achieve less.
Systems multiply but clarity dissolves.
Cost rises faster than revenue.
Leaders become tired instead of strategic.
Teams compensate through heroics, which later become resentment.

When the Vehicle is wrong, even brilliance becomes wasted effort.

Why 3XV Sits Above the Five Pillars

3XV is not a nice-to-have.
It is the structural blueprint for the entire organisation.

The Pillars, Systemisation, Staffability, Scalability, Sustainability, and Sellability, cannot fix identity problems.
They can only execute identity.

This is the mistake I see most often:
Leaders redesign processes, change structures, hire new people, or invest in technology, but they never re-architect the 3XV foundation.

When identity is wrong, the Pillars become overworked and under-effective.

Systemisation becomes bureaucracy.
Staffability becomes confusion.
Scalability becomes impossible.
Sustainability becomes firefighting.
Sellability becomes wishful thinking.

No Pillar can compensate for a broken 3XV.

The Moment Leaders Finally Understand

There is a specific moment, one I have witnessed in dozens of boardrooms, when a leader finally sees the fracture.
Their shoulders drop.
Their breathing shifts.
The room becomes still.

And they whisper some variation of:
"So the problem wasn't the people...
It wasn't the systems...
It wasn't the market...
It was us."

Not in a self-critical way, but in a self-aware way.

Because once a leader realises the identity was misaligned, they can finally rebuild the architecture without blame, without confusion, and without the emotional heaviness that comes from chasing symptoms.

What Happens When 3XV Is Right

Everything changes.

Vision gives the organisation direction.
Value gives it relevance.
Vehicle gives it momentum.

The Pillars begin to align effortlessly.

Systemisation clarifies flow.
Staffability strengthens the load-bearing structure.
Scalability becomes natural rather than forced.
Sustainability protects integrity.
Sellability becomes predictable.

Leaders stop firefighting.
Teams stop guessing.
Culture stops resisting.
The organisation stops feeling heavy.

When 3XV is right, effort decreases,
and results increase.

That is the paradox of identity-led architecture:
The clearer the foundation, the lighter the organisation becomes.

The Bridge Into Architecture

Everything you've read so far has been preparing you for what comes next.

3XV is the blueprint.
The Five Strategic Pillars are the architecture.

Identity without structure is fantasy.
Structure without identity is chaos.

When 3XV is wrong, nothing works.
When 3XV is right, everything finally begins to make sense.

And now, we move into Chapter 3, the moment where strategy meets structure and the real architectural work begins.

CHAPTER 3:
Translating 3XV Into Architecture

The Moment Strategy Meets Structure

There is a specific moment in every organisation when strategy, no matter how elegant, intelligent, or inspiring, collides with structure. It's the moment leaders realise that their ambition is no longer the issue. Their architecture is.

Most leaders don't notice this moment when it arrives. It appears quietly, disguised as operational friction: a delayed decision, a stalled project, a meeting that goes nowhere, a team that looks busy but achieves less. This friction is not incompetence. It is not resistance. It is not lack of accountability.

It is the sound of strategy hitting structural reality.

When I first learned to recognise this moment, it changed everything. It shifted the way I listened to leaders, the way I read boardrooms, the way I diagnosed problems. Until then, I believed what most people believe, that clarity creates execution. That if a strategy is clear enough, people will find a way to deliver it.

But I was wrong.
Strategy is the intention.
Structure is the permission.

A strategy can only travel as far as the architecture allows.

The Boardroom Where It Became Unmistakably Clear

It happened during a high-stakes strategic session for a multinational firm. The CEO was presenting a bold three-year vision, one that, on paper, was both inspiring and achievable. Their Value was strong. Their Vehicle was aligned. Their market position was enviable. Their ambition was credible.

But as he spoke, I watched the executive team very closely.

Some nodded.
Some took notes.
Some stared into the middle distance, doing silent calculations.

But one expression stood out:
the quiet panic of a leader who knows the strategy makes sense,
and knows the structure cannot deliver it.

When the CEO finished, the COO leaned back, folded his arms, and said nothing. It wasn't resistance. It was recognition. He knew, instinctively, that the current architecture could not carry the future being described.

The friction had arrived.
Not as an argument.
Not as a disagreement.
But as a mismatch between intention and capacity.

This is the structural truth I want you to understand:

Strategy becomes useless the moment it exceeds the integrity of your architecture.

It doesn't matter how brilliant the destination is if the organisation isn't designed to reach it. Strategy must be translated into systems, roles, rhythms, and decisions. Without structure, strategy becomes pressure, and pressure becomes drift.

The Leader Who Mistook Agreement for Alignment

A few years later, I was advising another company preparing for an ambitious expansion. Their Vision was clear. Their Value was validated. Their Vehicle was chosen. Everything appeared aligned. The CEO presented the strategy to his senior team, and everyone nodded in agreement. It felt like alignment.

But agreement is not alignment.
Alignment exists only when the structure supports the strategy.

Two weeks later, the first cracks appeared. Teams interpreted priorities differently. Departments made decisions based on historic habits rather than future design. Conflicting assumptions emerged. The architecture had not been redesigned to support the new direction, and so the old architecture began fighting the new strategy.

The CEO looked at me, confused.
"They agreed in the meeting," he said.
"Yes," I replied. "But the structure didn't."

People had not resisted.
The architecture had.

When a strategy is right but the structure is wrong, the organisation fights the leader, quietly, unintentionally, and relentlessly. Not because people lack commitment, but because the system defaults to what it was originally designed to do.

This is the moment where most leaders lose faith in their teams.
I tell them instead:
"Don't blame the behaviour.
Blame the architecture that created it."

The Most Expensive Strategy Mistake Leaders Make

The most expensive mistake I've seen in my entire career is this:

Leaders announce a new strategy without redesigning the structure that will deliver it.

They assume that the organisation can simply "try harder."
They assume people can "figure it out."
They assume the existing architecture can stretch.

But architecture does not stretch.
It breaks.

When leaders push strategy faster than structure, the cost is enormous:

- Decision fatigue

- Fractured priorities

- Leadership overload

- Cultural confusion

- Systemic bottlenecks

- Declining morale

- Wasted resources

- Missed opportunities

- And eventually, organisational drift

All because the strategy was never translated into architecture.

The Quiet Turning Point of Leadership Maturity

There is a point in every leader's journey, usually after their first major strategic failure, when they finally understand why architecture matters.

It is the moment they stop asking:
"How do we get people to deliver this strategy?"

And start asking:
"What architecture must exist for this strategy to be delivered effortlessly?"

This shift transforms everything.

Leaders stop pushing.
They start designing.

They stop complaining about behaviour.
They start strengthening systems.

They stop micromanaging.
They start architecting.

They stop firefighting.
They start predicting.

They stop forcing execution.
They start enabling it.

This is the moment a leader crosses the line from operational manager to organisational architect.

I've seen CEOs rise ten levels in effectiveness within weeks once they make this shift.

Why Most Leaders Never See This Moment Coming

Most leaders grow up inside operational cultures. They are trained to solve problems, make decisions, respond quickly, manage people, handle crises, and maintain performance. But they are rarely taught to design.

They inherit the architecture.
They operate it.
They optimise it.
 But they do not question it.

And because the architecture is invisible, they treat symptoms instead of root causes. They adjust processes, replace team members, redesign dashboards, add meetings, bring in new tools, but none of it creates real change because none of it touches the structure.

Architecture is silent.
Invisible.
Yet absolute.

It is the quiet dictator of organisational behaviour.

A Subtle Foreshadow: The Consequence of Speaking Truth Too Early

In my early career, I developed a habit that became both my curse and my gift. When I saw structural misalignment, when I saw strategy fighting architecture, I said it plainly. Too plainly. Too early. Too honestly.

And leaders weren't ready.

I paid for it with **27 firings** across my early consulting years.
But within three years, those same leaders rehired me **22 times**, because the architectural truth eventually revealed itself. They didn't fire me because I was wrong. They fired me because the truth arrived before their readiness.

This is the moment where strategy meets structure, where your ambition confronts your architecture. In the next section, we go deeper:

Why leaders resist the truth even when the structure is screaming it.
Why timing matters as much as accuracy.
And how speaking architectural truth too early shaped my entire career.

Why Leaders Resist the Truth

There is a particular kind of silence that fills a room when you speak a truth a leader is not yet ready to hear. I have felt that silence more times than I can count. And in my early career, I paid dearly for it.

I did not set out to become the man fired twenty-seven times.
Nor did I ever imagine that twenty-two of those same leaders would come back to me, often quietly, almost sheepishly, within three years.

But that journey became the curriculum that shaped the Strategic Architect I would eventually become.

The Curse of Seeing Too Early

People assume being able to see fractures early is an advantage. It is, but only if the leader is prepared for the truth. Early in my career, I didn't understand timing. I mistook clarity for correctness and correctness for readiness. I believed that if I saw a structural failure, it was my duty to name it immediately.

I was wrong.

A truth delivered too early can be more destructive than a lie delivered on time.

In those early years, I would walk into companies full of conviction. I'd analyse quickly, see patterns instantly, and give leaders the unfiltered truth. Not opinion. Not theory. Structural truth. The same truth they would discover months later, but truth they were not ready, emotionally or politically, to hear in the moment.

At the time, I thought I was being helpful.
What I was really being was premature.

People think leaders fear bad news.
They don't.
They fear truths that require identity change.

When you tell a leader their company is drifting, they brace.
When you tell a leader *they* are the drift, they break.

Most of my firings came not from what I said, but from what my words required them to confront.

The First Firing: A Truth Too Sharp

The first firing happened with a mid-sized firm that brought me in to advise on their expansion. Within a week, I realised they weren't ready to scale. Their systems couldn't carry the load, their leadership structure was confusing, and their Vision had drifted into contradiction.

I told the CEO plainly:
"You're expanding a company that isn't designed to be expanded."

He fired me that afternoon.

I walked out confused. I thought I had helped him. But what I had really done was expose a fracture he didn't yet have the emotional architecture to face.

Eight months later, as the company's growth stalled and internal tension rose, he called me back.

"I think I'm ready to hear the rest," he said quietly.

That was the first rehiring.
There would be twenty-one more.

The Next Twenty-Six Firings: Patterns of Resistance

Every firing had its own flavour, but the pattern was always the same:

1. **I saw the truth early.**

2. **I said it plainly.**

3. **It landed too close to someone's identity.**

4. **They removed me to remove the discomfort.**

I was dismissed for saying:

- "Your culture is producing the exact behaviour you claim to hate."

- "Your systems are encouraging drift, not preventing it."

- "Your leaders are busy, not aligned."

- "Your success is now your greatest structural risk."

- "You are growing faster than your architecture."

- "Your team is compensating for design flaws, not performance issues."

And the most painful one of all:
"You are the bottleneck."

Every time, the initial reaction was defensiveness, then rejection. In those years, I became familiar with quiet exits, awkward handshakes, and emails that said, "We've decided to take a different direction."

But the most painful truth was this:
I was right, but I was early.
And early truth is indistinguishable from threat.

The Emotional Cost of Being Early

Being fired repeatedly does something to you. You start doubting your instincts. You question whether you're too harsh, too direct, too uncompromising. You wonder why others can say softer things and get praised, while your clarity gets punished.

The turning point came when a seasoned executive pulled me aside after my seventh firing. He said something that changed my entire philosophy:

"Moe, your problem isn't that you're wrong. Your problem is that you tell the truth before the leader has a place to put it."

Those words shifted everything.

Truth needs a container, psychological, emotional, and structural.
Without it, even the most accurate insight feels like an attack.

This realisation is what transformed me from a consultant into an architect.

I stopped trying to *convince*.
I started trying to *prepare*.
I stopped leading with truth.
I started leading with clarity, then ease, then direction.
And when the truth finally landed, leaders could absorb it instead of defend against it.

The Rehirings: When Truth Becomes Inevitable

The first rehiring surprised me.
The second confused me.
By the tenth, I understood the pattern.

People don't return to someone who embarrassed them.
They return to someone who was right.

Sometimes it took a quarter.
Sometimes two years.
Sometimes a crisis.
Sometimes a competitor overtaking them.
Sometimes a failed initiative.
Sometimes a quiet, private admission that they could no longer pretend the fracture wasn't real.

Every one of the twenty-two rehirings began with a variation of the same sentence:

"Moe… you warned me."

The difference was that now they were ready.
They had felt the consequences of avoiding the truth.
They had hit the boundary of their current architecture.
They were no longer protecting identity, they were protecting survival.

When leaders become ready, truth becomes welcome.
What once felt like criticism becomes liberation.

What Those Years Taught Me About Human Architecture

Those firings taught me more about leadership psychology than any book, qualification, or workshop ever could.

They taught me that:

- **Leaders don't resist the truth, they resist the implications of the truth.**

- **People defend their identity more fiercely than their strategy.**

- **A leader's ego is often the last barrier to structural clarity.**

- **Timing is as important as accuracy.**

- **Truth without emotional preparation creates rejection, not change.**

- **Insight must be scaffolded, not hammered.**

- **Trust is not built by being right, it's built by helping leaders feel safe enough to see what they already know.**

The greatest lesson was this:

You cannot give a leader the truth.
You can only create the conditions where they choose to see it.

Once I understood this, my entire approach changed.
I stopped delivering architectural diagnoses like declarations.
I started leading leaders toward seeing their own structure.

This was the shift that eventually transformed my practice into the Strategic Architect model I use today.

The Deeper Truth Behind the 27 Firings

Looking back, I realise something even more profound:

Those leaders didn't fire me because I was wrong.
They fired me because I violated the order of transformation.

The order is simple:

1. **Safety**

2. **Clarity**

3. **Truth**

4. **Action**

5. **Architecture**

In my early years, I entered at step three, without providing steps one and two.
I delivered truth into a room without safety or clarity. I spoke from insight instead of empathy. I trusted my instincts more than their readiness.

Those firings were not punishments.
They were tuition.

They forced me to soften without weakening.
They taught me to sequence insight with emotional intelligence.
They helped me build a way of working that leaders could absorb instead of resist.

Today, I still give the same truths I gave back then,
but in the right order, with the right context, and at the right time.

And that difference is everything.

How These Scars Shape the Work I Do Now

The scars of those early years now shape every engagement I take on:

- I listen for readiness before delivering insight.

- I pace architectural truth with emotional capacity.

- I read the room before reading the strategy.

- I slow leaders down long enough for clarity to land.

- I design frameworks that make the truth feel safe to accept.

People sometimes ask how I developed the ability to sense fractures so quickly.

What they don't realise is that the ability came second.
The scars came first.

The Hard Lesson of Being Early

There is a particular kind of pain that comes from seeing the truth before everyone else. It is not arrogance, though others often assume it is. It is not ego, though it can trigger the egos of those who hear it. It is not even confidence, because confidence feels warm, and early truth feels cold.

The pain of being early is the pain of knowing what will break long before anyone else is willing to acknowledge it.

For years, I mistook this ability for a gift. Over time, I realised it was also a burden, a burden that shaped my career in ways I never anticipated. People remember the 27 firings. But what they don't see is the internal battle that came with them: the doubt, the questioning, the slow, difficult recognition that clarity without pacing can be dangerous.

Being early is lonely work.

The Uncomfortable Gift of Pattern Recognition

In my twenties and early thirties, my mind worked like a structural scanner. I could walk into a company and within days see the weight-bearing weaknesses, where the leadership load was too heavy, where decisions were bottlenecked, where culture contradicted strategy, where systems masked fractures instead of preventing them.

At first, I thought everyone saw what I saw.
They didn't.

Then I thought they couldn't see it.
Often, they could, but only emotionally, not structurally.

What I thought were insights felt like confrontations to others. What I believed were warnings felt like criticisms. What I thought were patterns felt like accusations.

I was speaking the language of architecture to leaders living in the language of operations.

They heard the words.
But not the meaning.

The First Time I Realised I Was Early, Not Wrong

The first time this truth hit me, truly hit me, was after one of my earliest dismissals. I had warned a leadership team that their growth model was unsustainable. They dismissed my concerns, thanked me politely, and ended the engagement. I walked out embarrassed.
But four months later, their COO called me privately.

"We didn't fire you because you were wrong," he said.
"We fired you because we weren't ready to hear how right you were."

That sentence cut through me.

It reframed every firing before it.
It reframed every firing still to come.

The problem wasn't the truth.
The problem was the timing.

Early Truth Threatens Identity

When you tell a leader the structure they built is failing, you're not critiquing their company, you're touching their identity. Leaders don't resist truth because they're stubborn. They resist it because it clashes with two internal forces:

1. **The identity they've built over years**

2. **The story they're telling themselves about the future**

Early truth disrupts both.

When I entered a room and said,
"This will break,"
what leaders heard was,
"You built something fragile."

When I warned,
"You're scaling a structure that cannot carry the weight,"
they heard,
"You misdesigned your own success."

No matter how elegant or accurate the insight was, early truth felt personal, not structural.

A leader must be emotionally ready to detach who they are from what they built. Until that happens, truth is a threat.

The Structural Cost of Being Early

What I eventually learned is that early truth can destabilise a company.

I once told a founder-run organisation that their leadership operating rhythm was the bottleneck. I was right, but early. They hadn't yet experienced the consequences of that bottleneck. They hadn't felt the repetition of mistakes, the pile-up of decision fatigue, the slow erosion of cultural confidence.

I was giving them chapter seven when they were emotionally still in chapter two.

Because of my premature honesty, they reacted defensively. Meetings became tense. Leadership alignment weakened. My presence became symbolic of pressure, not clarity.

They fired me within weeks.

A year later, after turnover issues, decision breakdown, and a failed product launch, they brought me back.

"We heard you," the founder said.
"But we needed the pain to understand the meaning."

That was the moment I realised the deepest lesson of all:

Truth without timing fractures alignment.
Truth delivered at the right moment accelerates transformation.

Why Being Early Shapes You More Than Any Failure

The more I was fired for being early, the more I began studying not just organisational architecture, but human architecture, the internal structures leaders rely on to make sense of difficult truths.

I learned that:

- People accept truth only when the cost of avoiding it exceeds the cost of facing it.

- Leaders need emotional space, not intellectual evidence.

- Timing is a structural component of influence.

- Insight must arrive at the speed of absorption, not the speed of recognition.

- Readiness is architectural, it has indicators, patterns, and conditions.

This understanding transformed my work. I no longer dropped truth into a room like a stone into still water. I prepared the surface. I built the psychological scaffolding. I led leaders toward their own realisations instead of handing them conclusions.

Early truth without sequence is brutality.
Early truth with sequence becomes revelation.

The Day I Stopped Trying to Be Early

There was a pivotal moment, after my twenty-something-th firing, when I sat in a café in London, staring at my notebook. I had written the same sentence three times:

"I am right, but I am early."

It was the first time I confronted the possibility that being right wasn't enough.
Architecture doesn't just need insight.
It needs timing, readiness, and emotional calibration.

That day, I made a commitment:

I will stop being early.
I will start being timely.

And that decision became the hinge on which my entire career turned.

When Early Truth Becomes Strategic Advantage

I still see the truth early.
That will never change.

But now I unveil it with intent, not impulse.
With empathy, not urgency.
With architecture, not impatience.

When leaders feel safe, they listen.
When leaders feel understood, they open up.
When leaders feel prepared, they transform.

The irony is this:
Once I learned to stop being early, leaders began inviting me earlier.

Not because I softened the truth,
but because I softened the moment.

CHAPTER 4:
SYSTEMISATION, THE FLOW-BEARING PILLAR

Why Flow Fails in Good Companies

Flow rarely collapses in weak companies. Weak companies never had flow to begin with.
Flow collapses in the good ones, the ambitious ones, the ones that grew faster than the architecture beneath them.

It's one of the hardest truths for leaders to accept, because when flow begins to fail, it doesn't announce itself with dramatic chaos. It arrives quietly, disguised as busyness. On the surface, the organisation looks alive. People rush from meeting to meeting. Slack messages explode through the day. Status updates grow longer. Dashboards fill with movement. But underneath all that activity, something essential is slipping.

Good companies are seduced by movement.
Movement feels like momentum.
Momentum feels like progress.
Progress feels like success.

But movement without coherence is drift.
And drift is the first sign of architectural failure.

I once worked with a £47M company that appeared, from the outside, to be running beautifully. Their people were sharp. Their culture was energetic. Their leadership team was admired. But as soon as I walked into the building, I felt something was off. It was in the hurried footsteps, the rapid-fire conversations, the stack of half-finished initiatives pinned to the walls. Everyone was working hard, harder than necessary, and yet the organisation felt strangely heavy.

When flow fails, the weight of the organisation shifts from the architecture onto the people. You can see it in their faces before you see it in the numbers.

They told me they were "just busy."
But busyness is never the cause.
It is always the symptom.

As I observed the company over the next few days, the fractures revealed
themselves slowly. Decisions moved upwards when they should have
travelled sideways. Conversations became diluted as they passed through
layers, losing sharpness with every retelling. Processes that once worked
smoothly had become tangled by improvisations created during periods
of fast growth, shortcuts taken during crises, temporary workarounds that
became permanent, small and subtle deviations that eventually hardened into
complexity.

What I was witnessing was not incompetence.
It was process debt, the accumulation of structural shortcuts created faster
than the architecture could absorb them.

Each shortcut made sense at the time. Each small deviation helped the team
survive a moment. But architecture doesn't forget. What you avoid fixing
accumulates silently, until the weight of past decisions begins to distort the
flow of the present.

In that same company, I watched as teams spoke more often yet understood
one another less. Communication increased in volume, but lost clarity with
every exchange. Leaders repeated priorities, but the message changed as
it travelled through the organisation, like a whisper passed along a line of
children who desperately want to get it right but have no structural way to
preserve the original meaning.

People were communicating constantly, but clarity was dissolving.
Noise had replaced signal.

The hardest challenge for the CEO was accepting that nothing he was
witnessing was a people problem. He believed his team had become
unfocused. Then he believed they weren't aligned. Then he believed they
weren't communicating well. Eventually he considered replacing several
managers.

But none of that was the truth.
The truth was far simpler, and far more structural:

The company's growth had outpaced its design.

Flow is not a behavioural issue.
Flow is architectural.

When a company grows faster than its systems, the structure begins to lag behind the ambition. At first, the gaps are small, a forgotten step here, a duplicated decision there, an unclear handoff, a meeting that accomplishes nothing because no one knows who truly owns the next step. One or two of these moments is nothing. But a thousand small frictions create a gravity that slows the entire organisation.

Eventually, even brilliant people look average.
Even committed teams appear overwhelmed.
Even strong leaders look reactive and fatigued.

This is the hidden cruelty of flow failure:
it makes good people look like the problem.

I remember walking through the operations floor of that company on my third day. Teams were in constant motion. Everyone seemed busy. Yet every task appeared to require more effort than it should. I watched one group spend twenty minutes clarifying who had authority to approve a simple request. In another department, I saw a project stalled because a bottlenecked leader had become the accidental owner of ten decisions that should never have reached him. The entire place was running on human effort rather than architectural ease.

When I met privately with the CEO, I explained what I saw.

"Your people are not failing," I said.
"They're compensating."

He leaned back in his chair, exhausted.
"I've been telling them to work smarter, not harder," he replied.
The sadness in his voice revealed that he no longer believed it himself.

"You don't have a people problem," I continued.
"You have a flow problem. And flow problems are structural, not behavioural."

What I didn't say, but what he eventually learned, is that flow failure is the most dangerous failure of all. It arrives slowly, invisibly, like hairline cracks in a bridge. At first, the weight is absorbed. Then the flex begins. Then the structure strains. Then one day, without warning, the entire load-bearing pathway gives way.

Good companies collapse not through chaos, but through erosion.

In the months that followed, we uncovered something profound: the flows inside the organisation, decisions, communication, and processes, had been designed for a £10M company, not a £40M one. Everyone was operating inside a structure that no longer matched reality.

Decision flow had become vertical, not lateral.
Communication flow had become noisy, not precise.
Process flow had become improvised, not intentional.

Their architecture was built for yesterday, yet expected to carry tomorrow.

That mismatch is the silent assassin of good companies.

Flow breaks not when people fail, but when the architecture forces them to work against the natural movement of the organisation. When decisions have nowhere clear to land, they bounce. When communication has no reliable channels, it scatters. When processes have no owner, they mutate.

The company had not created chaos.
It had inherited it.

When we finally redesigned the architecture, clarifying pathways, simplifying decisions, removing bottlenecks, reconnecting loops, something remarkable happened. The company did not feel faster. It felt lighter. People walked differently. Leaders breathed differently. Meetings shortened. Priorities sharpened. Work regained rhythm.

Flow had returned.

The CEO told me something at the end of that transformation that I've never forgotten:

"I thought we were slowing down because we needed to work harder. But we were slowing down because our architecture wasn't designed for who we had become."

That is why flow fails in good companies.
Not because they are broken, but because they have outgrown themselves.

And flow will always collapse in any organisation where yesterday's architecture is forced to carry tomorrow's ambition.

The Hidden Weight of Invisible Decisions

There is a moment in every growing company when leaders begin to feel something they cannot name. It is not chaos, not crisis, not even conflict. It is weight. A heaviness that creeps into the organisation one decision at a time.

No one sees it happening.
No one measures it.
But everyone feels it.

This weight is created by the most dangerous structural force inside any organisation: **invisible decisions**, decisions that have no clear owner, no defined pathway, no natural landing place, yet still demand to be made.

Invisible decisions are heavier than visible ones because they accumulate in silence. They travel through the organisation like unanchored currents, attaching themselves to whoever looks strongest in the moment. They land on leaders who are already overwhelmed. They sit with teams who do not have the authority to act. They bounce between departments like static electricity, draining clarity from every conversation they touch.

When invisible decisions accumulate, the organisation slows.
Not because people lack skill, but because the structure forces them to devote energy to what should never require effort.

I first understood this years ago while working with a company who believed they had a communication problem. They weren't communicating poorly, they were communicating constantly. Meetings multiplied. Emails overflowed. Slack channels grew by the day. People were drowning in information, not starved by it. Yet nothing moved faster. In fact, everything moved slower.

The real issue wasn't communication.
It was the hidden weight of invisible decisions travelling underneath it.

One morning, I sat silently in the corner of their leadership meeting, observing. The CEO asked a simple question: "Who approves the final pricing for this product?" Four people answered. All four gave different explanations. The CEO's expression tightened. It wasn't frustration, it was realisation. He had been assuming that clarity existed simply because he had once communicated it. But clarity does not endure without architecture. It dissolves under pressure and time.

Later that day, I walked through the operations floor and watched the same pattern unfold repeatedly. Decisions large and small floated in the air, waiting for someone, anyone, to grab them. A team leader would make a choice, only to learn hours later that a different leader had already reversed it. A simple question about next steps spiralled into a fifteen-minute search for who had authority. People were moving, but decisions were not.

Invisible decisions were consuming the organisation's oxygen.

The hidden cost of these decisions is enormous. Each one triggers hesitation. Hesitation triggers delay. Delay triggers confusion. Confusion triggers meetings. Meetings trigger misalignment. And misalignment triggers even more decisions, most of which should never have existed in the first place.

This is why leaders often say, "I feel like I'm making the same decision again and again."
They are.
Because the architecture forces them to.

Invisible decisions always rise to the top. They travel upwards by default, like heat in a building with no insulation. And when they reach a leader already carrying the weight of ten roles, they create structural stress that no amount of productivity, discipline, or motivation can offset.

I once watched a COO physically flinch when another department head approached him with what looked like a minor query. It wasn't the question that bothered him, he could have answered it in seconds. It was the cumulative weight of hundreds of such questions landing on him every month, slowly corroding his leadership bandwidth. His exhaustion wasn't a personal failure. It was architectural.

When decisions don't know where to go, they go to the busiest person in sight.

It's one of the slowest, quietest ways a company ends up with leadership bottlenecks, not because the leader is controlling, but because the structure is unclear. People default upward out of survival, not disempowerment.

I once asked a senior manager why she continued escalating decisions that should clearly have been made at her level. Her answer has stayed with me for years:
"I'm not sure anymore what belongs to me. And I can't afford to be wrong."

That sentence reveals everything about invisible decisions.
They don't create confusion.
They create fear of missteps.
And fear is the enemy of flow.

Fear forces people to wait.
Waiting creates backlog.
Backlog creates pressure.

Pressure creates urgency.
Urgency creates mistakes.
Mistakes create more decisions.

This is how companies exhaust themselves while appearing productive.

One of the most powerful transformations I ever witnessed occurred when a CEO finally understood this. For months he had been convinced his department heads lacked initiative. He insisted they should "step up," "take ownership," and "make decisions without asking." But the truth emerged slowly: they weren't lacking initiative. They were drowning under invisible decisions caused by missing pathways in the architecture.

His epiphany came during a conversation in his office.
He leaned back and asked me, "Why does everything still come to me?"
I answered gently, "Because the organisation doesn't know who else it belongs to."

He closed his eyes and nodded.
He wasn't disappointed in his team anymore.
He was disappointed in the architecture he had unknowingly created.

When we map decision pathways in organisations, something remarkable always happens. Leaders expect to find complexity. Instead, they find emptiness. Dozens of small but critical decisions with no owner. Major decisions with unclear criteria. Cross-functional decisions with no natural home. Strategic decisions that drift between leaders depending on who speaks first.

These gaps don't break a company immediately.
They corrode it gradually.

Invisible decisions steal hours, weaken clarity, dilute accountability, and force leaders to operate two levels below where they should be. They rob teams of confidence and rob the organisation of speed. They turn simple activities into multi-step processes and create the illusion of complexity where none should exist.

Flow collapses not because people lack capability, but because architecture lacks definition.

Years ago, I told a founder something that shocked him.
"You don't have a decision-making problem," I said.
"You have a decision-landing problem."

He laughed at first, then realised the truth. Decisions were being made, constantly, but they had nowhere to land. There was no structural holder

81

for them. So they bounced, ricocheted, or evaporated. And every time one dissolved, someone had to recreate it, usually badly, and usually under pressure.

The weight of invisible decisions does something even more destructive: it reshapes culture.
It makes people cautious.
It teaches them to wait instead of lead.
It trains them to ask instead of think.
It conditions them to escalate instead of resolve.
It builds a silent culture of dependency, not because people want to depend on leaders, but because the architecture forces them to.

When you remove invisible decisions, something beautiful happens.
The organisation exhales.

People rediscover clarity.
Leaders regain bandwidth.
Teams start moving with confidence.
Flow returns almost immediately, like water running through a pipe that was blocked for years.

And the surprising part?
It doesn't require heroics.
It requires architecture.

Design the decision pathways.
Clarify authority.
Name ownership.
Define landing places.

Once invisible decisions become visible, everything moves again.

Flow is not created by working harder.
Flow is created when decisions know where to go.

How 3XV Shapes Your Systems

When leaders think about systems, they often picture flowcharts, processes, software, automation, and documentation. They imagine structure growing upward from operations. But systems never begin at the operational level. They begin much higher, at the level of identity. They begin in Vision, Value, and Vehicle.

The system a company builds is not the system it needs.
The system a company builds is the system its identity demands.

Most leaders never see this connection. They treat their systems as operational necessities rather than architectural expressions. But systems are not neutral. They are shaped, often unconsciously, by the organisation's strategic identity.

I first understood this during a session with an eight-figure company in the Midlands. They were struggling with operational inconsistencies. Departments built their own workflows, customer experience varied wildly, and decisions were constantly revisited. At first, their executives assumed it was a documentation problem. Then a process problem. Then a management problem.

But none of those diagnoses were true.

Their systems were failing because their systems reflected their identity, or more accurately, the absence of one.

Their Vision wasn't sharp enough to shape how processes should move.
Their Value proposition had become fuzzy, so the organisation defaulted to whatever was most convenient.
Their Vehicle, a model that required speed and consistency, was being held within systems designed for deliberation and craftsmanship.

The systems weren't broken.
The identity was.

Every flow in the company was trying to serve a different interpretation of the future. And so, the systems became fragmented, contradictory, and unreliable, not because anyone had done anything wrong, but because nothing unified the organisational purpose.

When we clarified their 3XV, something astonishing happened. Without being told, teams began redesigning systems differently. Not randomly, but coherently. Decisions began landing in predictable places. Communication patterns started tightening. Processes shifted from improvisation to intention.

The architecture changed because the identity changed.

A Vision with sharp edges will always create systems with sharp edges.
A Vision that is foggy produces systems that drift.
A Vision without boundaries produces systems that collapse under flexibility.

One morning, as I sat with their senior operations team, I saw the first sign of structural change. They were mapping their customer journey, a task they had done many times before. But this time, they weren't asking, "What do we currently do?" They were asking, "What must we build to deliver the future we just committed to?"

That question, asked in that room, at that moment, revealed the structural truth leaders often miss:

Systems are not designed to support today.
Systems are designed to support tomorrow.

When Vision is unclear, every system becomes reactive.
When Vision is strong, every system becomes anticipatory.

Later that week, I met privately with the Head of People. She told me something I will never forget:
"For years, we've been designing roles around the skills people have. But now we're designing roles around the company we're becoming."

That shift, from reactive to purposeful, is the essence of how 3XV shapes systems.

I've seen companies build beautiful systems that collapse because the underlying identity is weak. I've also seen companies with minimal systems operate effortlessly because their identity is so sharp that almost every team subconsciously knows how things should flow.

Years ago, I worked with a founder-led organisation that had all the discipline you could hope for but none of the clarity required to make systems land. Their processes were documented meticulously. Their tools were world-class. Their operations manual was an object of pride. But the company struggled nonetheless. People didn't follow the systems. They improvised constantly. Teams created their own rules.

The founder believed it was a compliance issue.

It wasn't.
It was a Vision issue.

Their Vision changed every few months. It wasn't intentional, it was emotional. Whenever opportunity appeared, the direction shifted. Whenever a client asked for something new, the strategy adjusted. Whenever the founder felt inspired, the company took a different turn.

The systems weren't being ignored.
They were being contradicted.

When Vision moves faster than systems can stabilise, systems lose authority. People stop trusting the structure because the structure no longer reflects the path of the organisation.

When I finally showed the founder how his own shifting identity was reshaping, and ultimately undermining, the architecture, he fell silent. A long silence. The kind that means the truth has landed deeper than expected.

He whispered, "I thought our systems were resisting me."
I replied, "They weren't resisting you. They were protecting the organisation from ambiguity."

Systems are loyal to identity, not individuals.

A company cannot stabilise systems until it stabilises itself.
It cannot build flow until it builds clarity.
It cannot scale architecture until it scales purpose.

Another company, a rapidly scaling SaaS firm in London, taught me the opposite lesson. Their Vision was so sharp that systems became extensions of identity. Their processes weren't perfect, far from it, but the cohesion within them was extraordinary.

In one meeting, I watched an intern confidently refuse a request from a senior leader because, in her words, "that takes us away from the future we agreed to build." She wasn't being disrespectful. She was being architectural. The clarity in their 3XV was so strong that even the newest people in the organisation could sense when something was structurally misaligned.

That is the power of identity-led systems. When 3XV is strong, systems don't need enforcement. They gain gravity. People feel them rather than needing them spelled out.

A company's Vision shapes what systems must prioritise.
Its Value shapes what systems must protect.
Its Vehicle shapes how systems must operate.

Identity is the blueprint.
Systems are the expression.

When I explain this to leaders, many look stunned. They had assumed systems existed to create efficiency. But systems exist for something far deeper: to turn identity into architecture. To ensure that what the organisation believes is reflected in how it behaves.

Every breakdown in Systemisation, every delay, every bottleneck, every duplication, every misalignment, can be traced back to a conflict between identity and structure.

This is why some companies scale effortlessly while others suffocate under their own growth. The effortless ones don't have better systems. They have better identity alignment. Their 3XV provides the structural intelligence the architecture needs to remain coherent as the company expands.

The companies that suffocate aren't broken.
They are simply trying to carry tomorrow with systems built for yesterday.

A system cannot exceed the clarity of the identity it serves.
Flow cannot exceed the strength of the system that carries it.
And architecture cannot exceed the truth the organisation is willing to face.

This is why Systemisation is the first of the Five Pillars, because flow is where identity becomes structure. It is where intention becomes behaviour. It is where the vision stops being a story and starts becoming a system.

And in the next section, we step into the deeper truth:

Flow is not an accident.
Flow is built.
And it is built one architectural decision at a time.

The Dubai Flow Misdiagnosis

There are moments in my career that stay with me not because they were dramatic or emotionally charged, but because they revealed something about human nature that no framework ever could. One of those moments happened in Dubai, a place where ambition rises as quickly as the skyline, and where many leaders mistake movement for mastery.

The company was a rising star in the region, scaling fast, winning contracts others envied, and expanding into multiple markets simultaneously. From the outside, it looked unstoppable. Their brand was pristine, their energy infectious, and their hiring spree impressive. When they reached out to me, they framed the issue simply: "We need help improving communication. Things aren't flowing between departments."

That was the word they used, *flow*.
But they meant something entirely different.

I landed in Dubai on one of those warm evenings where the air feels thick with possibility. The CEO met me himself, a charismatic man in his forties who had built the company from three people to more than two hundred in less than five years. He exuded confidence, not arrogance, but the kind of confidence born from surviving battles others never saw.

As we drove from the airport to the hotel, he spoke rapidly, almost breathlessly, about the opportunities ahead, the partnerships in negotiation, the offices opening soon in Riyadh and Doha. Every sentence was fuelled by expansion. Growth was his oxygen.

But beneath the excitement, I sensed something else, a subtle edge in his voice.
A slight hesitation before certain phrases.
A flicker of something he couldn't admit yet.

Leaders rarely call me when they have a communication problem.
They call me when they have a structural one.
They just don't know it yet.

The next morning, I arrived at their headquarters, a beautiful glass building overlooking a busy boulevard. Inside, everything buzzed. Teams walked briskly, phones rang constantly, and the walls were adorned with strategy boards, launch plans, and timelines. At first glance, it seemed alive and dynamic.

But the busier a company looks, the stiller I become.
Movement is where flow hides, not where it lives.

I spent the morning quietly observing. Meetings were intense, full of ideas and debates. But something wasn't connecting. Every discussion orbited around the same themes: delays in execution, confusion about ownership, duplicated work, announcements that failed to reach the right people.

They believed this was a communication issue.
But communication issues are surface symptoms.
They are the smoke, not the fire.

During one meeting, I watched as a regional manager presented a new customer journey initiative. Halfway through, another manager interrupted, surprised, their team was already working on a similar project. A moment of awkwardness passed through the room. Neither department knew about the other's efforts.

The CEO laughed it off lightly.
"These things happen in fast-growing companies."

But his eyes told a different story, a story of a man realising for the first time that something deeper was wrong.

Later that afternoon, he invited me into his office, a spacious room overlooking the city, sunlight pouring through the glass. He leaned forward, elbows on his desk, the bravado of the previous day replaced by a quieter, more reflective tone.

"Moe," he said, "we're losing flow. Why is this happening now, when we're doing so well?"

I didn't answer immediately.
I've learned that silence is where truth gathers strength.

Finally, I said, "You're diagnosing the wrong problem."

He frowned slightly. "What do you mean?"

"Your organisation doesn't have a communication issue," I replied. "It has an identity issue. Your teams aren't out of alignment with one another. They're out of alignment with your 3XV."

He blinked, confused.
"3XV? We already have a clear Vision."

Most leaders believe they have a clear Vision.
What they really have is a sentence.

I asked him to walk me through his Vision. He spoke passionately for several minutes, growth targets, new markets, client categories, expansion timelines. There was ambition, but no architecture. Scale, but no shape. Movement, but no direction.

Then I asked about Value, why the market chose them. He paused. It was the first pause I'd seen in two days.
"Well... because we deliver fast," he said.

"That's not Value," I replied gently.
"That's a feature."

He exhaled, realising he wasn't as clear as he thought.

Finally, I asked about the Vehicle, the business model that carried the promise.

His answer was enthusiastic, but contradictory. He described three different approaches, each pulling the company in a different direction. At first, he didn't see the conflict. Many leaders don't. They confuse range with strategy.

When identity lacks coherence, systems compensate.
And when systems compensate, flow collapses.

We spent the next hour mapping the ripple effects. His Vision was interpreted differently by different departments. His Value proposition was assumed rather than defined. His Vehicle was flexible to the point of distortion. And because the identity was drifting, every system drifted with it.

Communication didn't fail.
Alignment did.

Execution didn't crumble.
Clarity did.

Flow didn't break.
Identity cracked.

That was the misdiagnosis, not a communication problem, but a coherence problem.

The next day, I ran a workshop with his executive team. I watched as they debated strategy with passion but without a unifying direction. Each leader had their own interpretation of the future. Each believed their version was correct. Each had built systems that reflected their own understanding of the company's identity.

The company didn't have one flow.
It had seven.
And none of them connected.

At one point, a senior manager asked, "How do we fix communication between departments?"
I turned to him and said, "Fix the identity they're all communicating from."

The room fell silent.

When identity becomes incoherent, flow becomes impossible.
Systems become fragmented.
Processes become inconsistent.
Teams become territorial.
Meetings become circular.
Communication becomes noisy.
Speed becomes illusion.

Later that afternoon, the CEO approached me privately.
"So the problem isn't Dubai?" he asked.

"No," I said. "Dubai is the stage. Your architecture is the script."

He nodded slowly.
It was the moment the misdiagnosis dissolved.

Over the next six months, the transformation was remarkable.
We sharpened their Vision until it had edges.
We clarified their Value until it had gravity.
We defined their Vehicle until it had discipline.

And once identity stabilised, flow returned almost effortlessly.

People didn't need more meetings, they needed a north star.
Teams didn't need more communication, they needed coherence.
Systems didn't need overhaul, they needed alignment.

Months later, the CEO told me something I still use in workshops.

"Moe, our systems didn't break because we scaled too fast.
They broke because we scaled without identity."

That sentence captured the entire lesson.

In Dubai, the misdiagnosis wasn't a mistake.
It was a mirror.

Good companies misdiagnose flow because flow hides its failures under the noise of activity. But once you strip away the noise, the truth is simple:

Flow is identity, expressed through architecture.
And identity, when fractured, will always make systems look guilty.

Your First Structural Clarity Question

There comes a moment in every mentoring relationship where the conversation moves from the organisation to the leader. Not in a dramatic, confrontational way, but in a quiet shift, a pause, a glance, a slow exhale, when the leader realises the architecture they're trying to fix on the outside is the same architecture they must examine on the inside.

This chapter has carried you through flow, identity, drift, and misdiagnosis. But none of it matters until you answer one question, the first question I ask every CEO who sits across from me, whether in London, New York, or a quiet corner office overlooking the desert in Dubai.

The question is simple.
But the answer never is.

The question is this:

"Where in your organisation does the weight always return to you?"

That's it.
Eight words.
But those eight words have softened leaders, shaken them, humbled them, and, more importantly, opened them.

Because weight does not lie.
Weight reveals architecture.

Whenever a company is stuck, overwhelmed, confused, or slowing, the weight eventually gravitates to its natural resting place. And that resting place is always structural, not accidental. The organisation is showing you, through pressure, where design has failed.

Some leaders answer immediately.
Others look away.
A few stare at the table for a long time before speaking.

But the most honest ones say, "I'm not sure yet. But I can feel it."

That response tells me everything I need to know. Feeling always precedes clarity.

Years ago, working with a fast-growing firm in Manchester, the CEO insisted he had no bottlenecks. "We're just busy," he kept saying. "Growing pains. Nothing unusual." But when I asked where the weight always ended up, he paused for the first time that day. He looked down at his inbox, thousands of unread messages. Then he looked at the doorway of his office, a steady stream of people waiting for approval, guidance, reassurance.

He whispered, "It always comes back to me."

There was no judgement in my silence. Only recognition. Every founder-driven business reaches this point. Once you scale beyond what instinct can carry, architecture must take over. But architecture cannot take over if all structural weight still lands on you.

I've had leaders tell me the weight returns through decisions.
Others say it returns through conflicts.
Others through customer escalations.
Others through operational breakdowns.
Others through financial clarity.
Others through team leadership.

Every answer is different.
But the pattern beneath them is always the same.

**Where weight collects
is where structure is weakest.**

Once you see this, everything changes.

One CEO once told me, "Moe, I feel guilty that everything comes to me." I corrected him gently: "It's not guilt. It's gravity. And gravity is architectural."

The weight does not reflect your weakness.
It reflects the organisation's design.

This is the first moment in the journey where the reader, you, must stop and look honestly at your own company. Not with frustration. Not with blame. Not with pride. With clarity.

Where does the weight always return to you?

Is it in decisions that should be distributed?
Is it in communication no one else seems able to anchor?
Is it in people problems that repeat in cycles?
Is it in operational drift you keep personally correcting?
Is it in financial oversight you cannot delegate?
Is it in strategic direction only you can hold?

If you cannot name the weight, you cannot redesign the architecture.
If you cannot locate the stress, you cannot relieve it.
If you cannot see the pathway, you cannot rebuild the flow.

This question matters because it begins the transition from surface solutions to structural thinking. It forces you to stop blaming symptoms and start recognising design. It shifts the conversation from "Why can't they?" to "Why must they?"
From "Why is this happening?" to "What have we built that makes this inevitable?"
From "Who's not performing?" to "What is the architecture compelling them to do?"

The Five Strategic Pillars will take you deeper, into Systemisation, Staffability, Scalability, Sustainability, and Sellability, but none of them can work until you face this first structural truth.

Weight is your compass.
Pressure is your teacher.
Gravity is your map.

So before we move forward, pause. Take a breath. Let your mind settle. And ask yourself again, without defence, without ego, without urgency:

Where does the weight always return to me?

Your answer is the doorway to the architecture your organisation truly needs.

CHAPTER 5:
Staffability, The People-Bearing Pillar

People Do Not Fail, Architecture Fails Them

There is a moment in every organisation, sometimes quiet, sometimes dramatic, when leaders begin to whisper about someone "not being good enough." They don't always use those words. Sometimes it's softer: *"They're struggling."* Sometimes harsher: *"They're not delivering."*
And sometimes it's disguised as empathy: *"Maybe they're just not the right fit anymore."*

But almost always, the leader speaks as if the problem lives inside the person.

I have spent forty years walking into companies at the exact point when these whispers become narratives, and narratives become decisions. And after all those years, here is what I know to be true:

People rarely fail on their own.
They fail inside an architecture that sets them up to fail.

This is not a romantic idea. It is structural reality.

Every behaviour you see, hesitation, overwhelm, inconsistency, resistance, disengagement, is an expression of architecture. People behave according to the system they are inside, the clarity they are given, the load they are carrying, and the flow that surrounds them.

When leaders tell me, "We have a people problem," I always ask the same question:

"Or do you have an architectural problem that looks like a people problem?"

Most of the time, the answer becomes clear within minutes.

The Myth of the Failing Employee

Years ago, I worked with a company in Leeds where one particular employee, a middle manager, had become the source of increasing frustration. Every leader had a story about him, slow responses, inconsistent decisions, teams that seemed disengaged under his watch. By the time I arrived, they had already begun discussing alternatives, perhaps moving him aside, perhaps replacing him.

On my second day with the company, I asked to shadow him quietly. What I saw was not incompetence. It was architectural cruelty.

He received contradictory instructions from three different leaders. He was expected to deliver results but had no authority over the teams whose cooperation he needed. The data he relied on was inconsistent across departments. His processes were outdated, built for a version of the company that no longer existed. His calendar was filled with meetings he didn't need to attend, yet these meetings consumed the very time he needed for the work he was evaluated on.

He wasn't failing.
He was drowning.

The organisation had placed him at the intersection of multiple structural fractures, unclear authority, broken communication loops, legacy processes, and leadership drift. He was carrying the weight of gaps he did not create.

His performance review told a story of underachievement.
 His architecture told a story of misdesign.

When I shared my findings with the executive team, the room fell silent. Not because they were defensive, but because they recognised the truth instantly.

They had been evaluating a man.
But the man was carrying the design.

The Unspoken Exhaustion of Good People

If you observe closely, you will see that most people who "fail" inside organisations are not defiant or lazy. They are exhausted. Exhaustion is the final symptom of architectural misalignment.

Exhaustion reveals:

- systems that fight instead of support

- communication that confuses instead of clarifies

- roles that expand without boundaries

- expectations that grow without design

- responsibilities that accumulate without authority

- decisions that land everywhere except where they belong

These conditions weaken even exceptional performers.
Architecture wears them down until they no longer recognise their own potential.

I once spoke to a talented leader who had been demoted after a series of failed initiatives. As he recounted what happened, he said something painfully honest:

"I never had a chance to succeed. I was always catching up to something broken."

The room he was sitting in wasn't broken.
The structure he was working inside was.

People become "difficult" when their architecture becomes impossible.
People become "underperformers" when clarity becomes optional.
People become "unmotivated" when success becomes unpredictable.

And people become "resistant" when the system forces them to protect themselves rather than perform.

These are not character flaws.
These are architectural outputs.

The Weight Leaders Accidentally Create

In many companies, leaders inadvertently create the very failure they later judge. Not out of malice, but out of speed, assumptions, and blind spots. When decisions are inconsistent, when priorities shift weekly, when processes change without context, when teams must compensate for unclear direction, the weight lands on the people.

I've seen leaders say, "They need to be more proactive," when the architecture punishes initiative.

I've seen leaders say, "They need to think for themselves," when decisions are routinely overridden.

I've seen leaders say, "They need to take ownership," when ownership is never structurally defined.

I've seen leaders say, "They're not leaders," when the operating rhythm gives them no space to lead.

People aren't resisting you.
They're resisting the confusion created by the structure around them.

In London, I worked with a scaling company where the CEO kept repeating, "I need my managers to step up." But what he really needed was an architecture that allowed them to step up, clear decision rights, clean reporting pathways, a consistent operating rhythm, and a system that rewarded leadership instead of firefighting.

When we rebuilt that architecture, the same managers he once doubted became the backbone of the company's next phase of growth.

People didn't change.
Structure did.

The Human Cost of Architectural Blindness

When architecture fails, it doesn't just damage performance.
It damages identity.

I've seen confident managers become hesitant.
I've seen creative thinkers become defensive.
I've seen high performers begin to question their worth.
I've seen teams turn inward to protect themselves from external chaos.
I've seen leaders withdraw emotionally because the structure punishes clarity.

When architecture fails, people begin rewriting stories about themselves:
"I'm not good enough."
"I'm the problem."
"I'm losing it."
"I'm falling behind."
"I'm not meant for leadership."

Those stories are rarely true.
But architecture makes them believable.

I once told a CEO something that surprised him:
"You don't fix people by developing them.
You fix people by unburdening them."

He paused for a long time, then whispered, "We've been doing the opposite."

The Moment Leaders Finally See It

There is always a moment, a personal, often painful moment, when a leader sees the truth. It is never during a report or a metrics review. It is always in a sudden flash of recognition.

Sometimes it happens when they witness a talented employee struggle with something that should be simple.
Sometimes it happens when they realise they themselves are carrying weight the structure should carry.
Sometimes it happens when they see the same patterns repeat across different people.
Sometimes it happens when they look at the organisation as a whole and see exhaustion instead of momentum.

In that moment, a leader finally understands:

People are not the architecture.
Architecture is what shapes the people.

And that is the moment true Staffability begins, not as an HR initiative, but as structural redesign.

When leaders commit to Staffability, they commit to creating an environment where people can succeed because the architecture allows them to. A place where clarity flows, roles make sense, authority matches responsibility, systems lighten the load rather than add to it, and the structure amplifies the individual's capability instead of draining it.

Staffability is not about staffing.
It is not about hiring.
It is not about performance management.

Staffability is the architecture of human success.

The Structural Truth That Changes Everything

After forty years of watching organisations rise, stall, collapse, and rise again, this is the truth that remains:

People do not fail.
They reveal where your architecture has failed them.

Once you see this, you can no longer lead the way you once did.
You stop blaming the individual.
You start examining the design.

You stop asking, "Why aren't they performing?"
You begin asking, "What in our architecture makes this performance impossible?"

You stop seeing talent as fixed.
You start seeing structure as fluid.

You stop trying to hire your way out of problems.
You start designing your way out of them.

This is the shift from managing people to architecting environments.

And once a leader makes that shift, their organisation will never operate the same way again.

The Leadership Load I Ignored Until It Hurt Us

There are mistakes you make early in your career that fade with time, and there are others that stay with you forever. This one stayed. Not because it was dramatic or public, but because it revealed something about leadership load that I had been blind to, something I should have understood, but didn't. Something that, for a time, hurt the people around me.

It happened years ago, before my work carried the weight it does today, before the Strategic Architect identity had fully formed. I was building a consulting practice that was growing faster than I expected. Momentum was on our side. Clients were calling. The work felt meaningful. My small team, talented, committed, and far more patient than I deserved, was doing everything in its power to keep pace.

But I didn't see the load they were carrying.
Because I wasn't watching the architecture.
I was watching the results.

I remember standing in our office late one evening, feeling pleased with what we had achieved that quarter. The numbers looked strong. The clients were renewing. The reputation was growing. And in that strange intoxication that comes from success, I assumed everything beneath me was just as strong.

I believed my team was coping, because they never complained.
I believed our systems were supporting them, because the work was getting done.
I believed I was leading well, because outcomes looked positive.

I was wrong on all three.

The truth made itself known slowly, in small signs that I ignored at first: a hesitation in someone's voice, a missed internal deadline, a quiet fatigue creeping into conversations. Nothing dramatic. Nothing that suggested collapse. Just small fractures invisible to a leader who wasn't yet trained to see architecture through human behaviour.

One afternoon, while preparing for a major client engagement, I noticed one of my team members, the one who normally carried a sense of calm competence, staring at her screen with a stillness I didn't recognise. Not focus. Not concentration. Stillness that comes from emotional overload.

"Are you alright?" I asked.

She nodded too quickly.

Too practiced.
Too polite.

Later that day, another team member came to me with a question he should never have had to ask, a question that revealed a missing system, a broken handoff, and an invisible weight he had been quietly compensating for.

"Who owns this part of the workflow?" he asked.

I paused longer than a leader should.
Because I didn't know.
Because I had never designed it.

I had assumed ownership would "naturally" emerge.
But ownership never emerges naturally.
Ownership is architectural.

That night, long after everyone left, I stayed in the office, lights dim, the hum of the air conditioning louder than usual, the room filled with that particular silence that only exists when truth is circling the perimeter, waiting for you to turn toward it.

For the first time, I saw the structure I had built through their eyes.

I saw the missing processes.
I saw the unclear boundaries.
I saw the decisions that had no landing place.
I saw the handoffs that relied on good intentions instead of design.
I saw the load I had unknowingly placed on people who trusted me.

I had been telling myself the team was strong.
What I should have been asking was whether the architecture was strong.

And then the deeper truth emerged, slowly but unmistakably:

Their load was rising because I wasn't carrying mine.

Not the work. I was working hard.
Not the hours. I was present.
Not the effort. I gave everything I had.

But I wasn't carrying the architectural load.
I wasn't designing clarity.
I wasn't defining roles properly.
I wasn't stabilising the operating rhythm.
I wasn't building systems to protect them from me.

I had created a structure where my speed became their burden.

My improvisation became their chaos.
My ambition became their exhaustion.

That night, I felt something I hadn't felt before, an ache of responsibility that was not about guilt but about recognition. Leadership is not about how much weight you can carry. It's about how much unnecessary weight you eliminate for others.

And I had failed at that.

I realised then that leadership load is not measured in effort.
It is measured in architecture.

Your people feel the quality of your design before they feel the quality of your intentions. My intentions had been noble. My architecture had not.

The turning point came a few weeks later. We were preparing for a major strategy workshop with a client in London. The pressure was high, and the workload even higher. My team was doing what they always did, delivering, compensating, pushing through.

But something in me had shifted.

Instead of asking, "Is the work done?" I asked, "What is the structure carrying? What is the team carrying? And what should the architecture be carrying instead?"

That question changed everything.

I began redesigning ownership with clarity.
I stabilised handoffs.
I removed decisions that didn't belong where they had accumulated.
I rebuilt the workflow so people could succeed by design, not by resilience.

I didn't tell the team I was doing this.
They simply felt the pressure ease.

One morning, months later, one of them said quietly, "It's different now. I can think again." That sentence will stay with me for the rest of my career.

Leadership load is not visible on dashboards.
It is revealed in the tone of someone's voice when they say, "I'm fine," and you know they're not.

It shows in the hesitation before they commit.
In the tiredness behind their eyes.
In the way they avoid asking for help because the structure has taught them the cost of asking is higher than the cost of absorbing.

That experience changed me.
It softened me.
It sharpened me.
It forced me to confront the truth I now teach everywhere:

You are not responsible for carrying the organisation's weight.
You are responsible for designing how the organisation carries weight.

Leaders often underestimate how architecture determines human experience. They believe people struggle because they are weak, distracted, or misaligned. But people struggle because the structure around them forces them to carry loads they were never designed for.

I learned this the hard way, by hurting people I never intended to hurt, simply because I had not learned how to protect them with architecture.

And that is why Staffability is the second Pillar.
Because once you see how architecture shapes people, you will never blame effort again.

DECISION LOAD

CEO   COO   CFO   OPERATIONS PRODUCT

The Kolbe Conative Architecture:

Mapping Human Load and Role Fit

There is a truth about people that every leader eventually discovers, usually after a painful and expensive lesson:
skill is not destiny, personality is not performance, and experience is not behaviour under load.

People do not show you who they truly are in interviews.
They show you who they want to be.

But the moment pressure arrives, real pressure, the kind that bends timelines and tests resolve, they default to one thing only:

their conative wiring.
Their instinctive mode of action.
The way they take initiative when no one is watching.

This is why I tell leaders:

> "You never fail because of who a person is.
> You fail because of where you put them."

Colleagues are not failing.
The architecture around them is failing *them*.

And no tool has helped me reveal this invisible structural truth more consistently than the **Kolbe A Index**.

Kolbe tells me how a person moves under load.
Where they accelerate flow.
Where they quietly become a bottleneck.
Where they burn out.
Where they carry the weight that others drop.

Kolbe is not personality.
It is not IQ.
It is not emotional literacy.
Kolbe measures **conation**, the architecture of instinctive doing.

In simple terms:
It reveals a person's natural operating system.

And once you know someone's operating system, you finally understand where they fit, where they thrive, and where they break.

The Brilliant Hire Who Broke the Team

ears ago, I advised a fast-growing company with a leadership team that looked perfect on paper, polished, experienced, and articulate.
But the CEO kept saying, "Something doesn't feel right. Our meetings drag. Our handoffs are slow. Decisions circle instead of moving forward."

I sat with the leadership team for a single day and watched their body language. That is all I needed.

Within hours, I could see it clearly:
the entire team was structured against their natural conative grain.

They had:

- a visionary CEO with a high Quick Start, constantly introducing new ideas,

- an operations lead who was a high Fact Finder and low Follow Thru,

- a CFO who was extremely low Follow Thru and low Implementor,

- and a commercial director whose Kolbe profile made them allergic to detail.

The result?

Meetings were not meetings, they were **friction maps**.
Everyone was working *against* their instinctive strengths.

The team was not broken.
The architecture was.

Kolbe revealed the truth instantly:
the CEO had hired impressive people for the wrong seats.

Once we redesigned the structure around their conative strengths, decision flow doubled, tension halved, and results improved almost immediately.

That was the day the CEO realised:
"You didn't fix the people. You fixed the architecture."

Exactly.

The Four Action Modes — Through an Architectural Lens

Kolbe breaks instinctive behaviour into four modes, but I never explain them like the textbooks.
I explain them like a Strategic Architect.

Because these four modes are **load-bearing behaviours**, not preferences.

1. Fact Finder, The Depth Engine

This shows how a person handles **detail, analysis, precision**.
High Fact Finders drill deep.
Low Fact Finders simplify fast.

One is not better, they simply carry different types of structural load.

2. Follow Thru, The Sequence Engine

This determines how someone manages **order, systems, processes, and structure**.
High Follow Thru stabilises flow.
Low Follow Thru adapts flow.

Put a low Follow Thru in a process-heavy role and they break.
Put a high Follow Thru in a chaotic environment and they break.

3. Quick Start, The Innovation Load Engine

This reveals tolerance for **risk, uncertainty, change**, and experimentation.
High Quick Starts thrive in ambiguity.
Low Quick Starts prefer predictability.

When mismatched, chaos emerges quickly.

4. Implementor, The Tangible Problem-Solving Engine

This reflects how someone handles **space, tools, and physical solutions**.
High Implementors think in models and physical alignment.
Low Implementors operate cleanly in the abstract.

These four modes are not preferences, they are **structural truths**.

When a team's conative wiring does not match the load path of the business, you get drift, friction, and silent failure.

The Four Seat Scenarios Every Leader Must Understand

There are four scenarios in Staffability, and nearly all team dysfunctions fall into one of them.

Understanding these is essential for any eight- or nine-figure company.

1. Right Person → Wrong Seat

The person is brilliant, but their Kolbe is incompatible with the seat's core load.

They are:

- overwhelmed

- stressed

- inconsistent

They blame themselves, but the structure is at fault.

This is the most common failure I see in fast-growth companies.

2. Wrong Person → Right Seat

The seat is designed correctly.
The architecture is sound.
But the person's conative wiring is misaligned.

They:

- cannot carry the load

- require constant management

- drain leadership bandwidth

This is more expensive than leaders admit, because the architecture itself is correct, but the human load cannot sustain it.

3. Wrong Person → Wrong Seat

This is where everything collapses.

The person is misaligned *and* the role is poorly defined.

This scenario creates:

- cultural drift

- political tension

- operational friction

- hidden decision bottlenecks

- disguised resentment

Most companies have at least one of these, usually in a senior role.

And everyone knows it, but no one speaks it.

4. Right Person → Changing Seat

This is the scenario almost no leader anticipates.

A high-performing team member begins struggling **only because the company has evolved**.

The role has changed.
The load has changed.
The speed has changed.
The complexity has changed.

But the person's Kolbe, their conative wiring, has not.

This is not failure.
This is evolution.

I've watched brilliant operational leaders break under the weight of a scaling company simply because the structure outgrew their natural instinct.

And the tragedy is:
they often believe it is their fault.

It isn't.
The architecture changed, not the person.

My Personal Kolbe Failure

Let me tell you one of my own mistakes.

Years ago, I hired someone who was charismatic, sharp, and highly experienced. I ignored my instinct, and worse, I ignored their Kolbe.

They were a high Quick Start, low Follow Thru.
The role required sustained structure, sequencing, and operational stability.

Within months, deadlines slipped.
Projects drifted.
I found myself doing their job for them.

But the real failure was mine.
I asked them to carry a load they were never designed to carry.

When I finally moved them to a more innovation-heavy role, they flourished.

The lesson?

People rarely fail.
Roles fail people.

Kolbe had shown me the truth from day one.
I simply refused to listen.

How I Use Kolbe in Eight- and Nine-Figure Organisations

When I enter a business, I look at Kolbe before I look at performance reports.

Why?

Performance shows the past.
Kolbe shows the truth.

Kolbe tells me:

- where the team will break

- where the drift originates

- where friction is inevitable

- where leadership bandwidth is being consumed

- which roles are structurally fragile

- which people are carrying heroic loads that will eventually crush them

I do not use Kolbe like a personality test.
I use it like a **load path diagnostic**.

Your team is an internal architecture.
Kolbe shows where the beams are aligned, and where the structure is carrying weight it cannot sustain.

3XV and Conative Architecture

Kolbe comes alive when integrated into your 3XV:

Vision

What kind of conative energy does the future require?

Value

Which instincts strengthen your point of differentiation?

Vehicle

Does your delivery model require more Fact Finders?
More Quick Starts?
More Follow Thrus?

Once you understand the future, you can architect the team that will carry it.

This is how identity drives talent architecture.

Reflection — Moe's Mirror

- Where in your organisation is a brilliant person carrying the wrong load?

- Where have you placed someone into a role that punishes their natural instinct?

- Which seats have evolved, but the people in them have not?

- And most importantly, where is your structure failing your people, not the other way around?

You cannot scale a business that misplaces its talent.

You cannot build resilient architecture with misaligned beams.

And you cannot expect people to carry loads their conative wiring will never sustain.

Staffability begins the moment you decide to **align human instinct with architectural design**.

Everything else is drift.

How 3XV Determines Talent Structure

Most leaders believe talent structure is built from skills, experience, and personality. They think roles emerge from operational need. They imagine team design as an HR exercise, a puzzle of competencies and availability.

But talent structure does not begin with people.
It begins with identity.

A company's 3XV, its Vision, Value, and Vehicle, shapes the architecture of talent long before a job description is written or a recruitment process begins. 3XV decides what kind of people the organisation needs, what roles must exist, what leadership layers are essential, what behaviours matter, and what structures will fail under pressure.

When 3XV is unclear, talent becomes random.
When 3XV is sharp, talent becomes inevitable.

I learned this the hard way through years of watching companies hire brilliant people into the wrong architecture, people who later appeared incompetent, resistant, or misaligned simply because the structure they were placed into did not match the identity of the organisation.

One particular engagement in Abu Dhabi made this lesson unmistakable.

The company had grown rapidly and decided it needed "senior talent" to take them to the next level. They hired aggressively, experienced leaders from global firms, specialists with strong résumés, and managers who had excelled in other industries. On paper, it was a dream team.

But within months, friction appeared everywhere.
Leaders clashed.
Teams hesitated.
Deadlines slipped.
Meetings grew heavier.

The CEO believed he had a culture problem.
He didn't.
He had an identity problem.

I sat with him one evening overlooking the city as the sun disappeared behind the skyline. He leaned forward and said, "Why can't these people work together? They're all so capable."

"They are capable," I replied softly. "But they're working inside a structure built without a clear identity. You hired individuals. You didn't hire architecture."

He frowned, confused.
"Explain."

So I began where every true talent design begins, with identity.

When Vision Is Unclear, Roles Become Overloaded

Their Vision was broad, ambitious, inspiring, but blurry. It aimed everywhere and nowhere at once. The company spoke about innovation, expansion, market leadership, differentiation, operational excellence, and customer obsession, all noble ideas, but none sharp enough to define how the organisation must behave tomorrow.

A blurry Vision creates blurry roles. People don't know whether they are building, protecting, scaling, or stabilising. When Vision has no edges, talent collapses under the weight of mixed expectations.

Some leaders pushed for speed. Others pushed for caution.
Some prioritised innovation. Others prioritised consistency.
Some built systems. Others bypassed them.

Each group believed they were right.
Each group *was* right, according to their interpretation of the Vision.

This is how brilliant people end up looking misaligned.
It is not the people.
It is the architecture they are placed inside.

When Value Is Undefined, Behaviours Become Inconsistent

The company's Value proposition was equally vague. They wanted to be "trusted partners" and "industry leaders", phrases that sound good in meetings but carry no operational meaning.

Value determines which behaviours matter.
It tells teams what to amplify and what to ignore.
It decides what excellent looks like.

Without a sharp Value proposition, leaders reward the wrong behaviours, tolerate the wrong patterns, and measure the wrong outcomes. In Abu Dhabi, some new hires believed speed mattered most. Others believed quality mattered most. Others focused on relationships. Others on innovation.

They weren't disagreeing.
They were serving different imagined versions of Value.

Architecture collapsed because Value was not a single truth, it was five competing beliefs.

When Vehicle Is Not Defined, Capabilities Become Mismatched

The company's business model, their Vehicle, had been evolving so rapidly that no one had paused to define what capabilities it actually required. They had built an engine on the move, hoping the right talent would simply adapt.

But Vehicle is destiny.
It dictates the structure of teams.
It defines what roles must exist and what roles are unnecessary.
It determines what leadership layers are essential and which ones will become bottlenecks.

When Vehicle changes, talent must change with it.
But in this company, roles remained anchored to an older model, one built for craftsmanship, not scale.

They had hired big-company leaders into a small-company Vehicle.
And small-company executors into a big-company ambition.
No one was wrong.
Everyone was mismatched.

It wasn't a talent issue.
It was a Vehicle issue.

3XV Reveals the People You Truly Need

When we rebuilt their 3XV, the talent picture transformed. Suddenly, we could see which roles were unnecessary, which ones needed to be created, which behaviours mattered, which ones needed to be eliminated, and which leaders belonged in an architecture designed for speed, scalability, and precision.

As we reshaped the identity, something remarkable happened.
The team began to self-sort.

Some leaders leaned in, finally understanding the company's direction with clarity.
Others stepped aside quietly, relieved to admit the role no longer aligned with who they were.
And some, who had been struggling for months, suddenly came alive, because the architecture now supported the work they were meant to do.

Talent becomes clear when identity becomes truth.

A Conversation I Never Forgot

One of the executives, a man who had struggled since the day he joined, asked for a private meeting. He sat down and said softly, "I thought I was failing."

"You weren't," I replied. "You were building for a version of the company that didn't exist anymore."

His eyes softened, but not with sadness, with release.

When 3XV is undefined, people think *they* are the problem.
When 3XV becomes sharp, they finally understand the structure they were trapped inside.

The Structural Truth Leaders Must Accept

The more years I spend working with leaders, the more convinced I become of this:

You don't hire people to fit the organisation.
You design the organisation to fit the identity.
And only then do you hire people who fit the identity's structure.

Vision determines which roles should exist.
Value determines which behaviours matter.
Vehicle determines the shape of the entire talent engine.

Once 3XV becomes coherent, talent becomes architectural.
People stop compensating for the structure.
The structure begins carrying them.

Only then does Staffability become real.

The Hiring Mistake That Cost Millions

There are mistakes you grow from, and there are mistakes that grow inside you. This one still sits with me, not because of the financial cost, though it was significant, but because it revealed something about hiring that I had been blind to at the time.

It happened more than twenty years ago, long before I had refined the frameworks I use today. Back then, I believed a strong hire could fix almost anything. Experience, pedigree, intelligence, I believed the right person in the right role could stabilise any structure.

I didn't yet understand that **a role is only as strong as the identity that shapes it**.

The company was a British firm expanding aggressively into Europe. They were convinced they needed a heavyweight leader, someone with gravitas, global experience, and strategic pedigree. A "name," as the chairman put it. They believed this hire would accelerate their growth, command investor confidence, and professionalise the leadership team.

I agreed.
That was my mistake.

The candidate they found was impressive. His résumé read like a greatest-hits collection, international leadership roles, major transformations, high-stakes decision-making. He had the calm confidence of someone accustomed to large rooms and large responsibilities.

During the interview process, I felt a quiet hesitation, a sense that his style didn't match the organisation's rhythm. But I ignored it. I mistook pedigree for alignment. I mistook credentials for architecture. I mistook experience for fit.

He was hired within weeks.
And the organisation changed instantly.

At first, everything looked promising. The leadership team was energised. The board felt reassured. The new hire took control quickly, reorganising departments, reallocating responsibilities, and implementing the systems he believed were necessary for scale.

But something strange began happening almost immediately.

The organisation slowed.

Not dramatically, subtly.
Meetings became longer.

Decisions became heavier.
Communication became more formal.
People became more cautious.

At first, the board interpreted this as professionalism. They believed the company was maturing. But within three months, cracks began to show.

Projects that once moved in weeks now dragged across quarters. Middle managers felt disempowered. Teams whispered that they no longer understood what "good" looked like. A culture once defined by agility now moved like an entity twice its size.

The most telling moment came during a strategy session when one of the frontline leaders said, half-joking but not really joking,
"We used to run. Now we wait."

That sentence sliced through the room.

By the sixth month, revenue had stalled. By the ninth, key clients were expressing frustration. By the twelfth, the organisation was haemorrhaging opportunities it would previously have captured with ease.

It took a year, a costly year, for everyone, including me, to see the truth clearly:

We didn't hire the wrong person.
We hired the wrong architecture.
And then placed a person inside it.

The new leader hadn't failed.
He had behaved exactly as someone from his identity, background, and context would. He brought big-company processes, expecting a big-company rhythm. He built layers where the organisation needed flexibility. He formalised systems that were not ready to be formalised. He introduced governance into a structure that still required agility.

He didn't misunderstand the organisation.
The organisation misunderstood itself.

The company's Vision wasn't defined enough to shape his decisions.
Its Value proposition wasn't clear enough to shape his priorities.
Its Vehicle wasn't mature enough to justify the architecture he was imposing.

He was building a cathedral.
They needed scaffolding.

He wasn't the problem.
The hire was premature.

The identity was incomplete.
The architecture wasn't ready.

And the millions they lost didn't come from his presence,
they came from our assumption that talent can compensate for structural absence.

I remember the day he resigned. He asked for a private meeting and spoke with sincerity, not frustration.

"Moe," he said, "I don't know what you want me to build here."

In that moment, the entire mistake crystallised.
We hadn't given him identity.
We had given him ambiguity.
We had placed him in a role that didn't yet structurally exist, a role he had to invent as he went, inside an organisation that couldn't absorb the architecture he was trying to create.

He left gracefully.
The company recovered slowly.
But the lesson changed me permanently:

Hiring decisions are not talent decisions.
They are identity decisions.

You cannot hire someone to shape what you haven't defined.
You cannot hire someone to stabilise what you haven't designed.
You cannot hire someone to lead where there is no architectural pathway for leadership.

When 3XV is unclear, even the most exceptional hire will fail.
When 3XV is sharp, even developing leaders can thrive.

Years later, when advising another CEO, I told him what I wish I had told that board in those early days:

"Do not hire for the company you dream of.
Hire for the identity you have the courage to commit to."

That is the structural truth that saved me from repeating the same mistake twice, and the truth that has saved leaders millions since.

CHAPTER 6:
SCALABILITY, THE GROWTH-BEARING PILLAR

Why Eight-Figure Companies Hit Invisible Ceilings

The first time I saw an eight-figure company hit its ceiling, I didn't recognise it. I was still early in my journey, still believing growth slowed because markets softened, competitors strengthened, or teams lost discipline. Those explanations felt reasonable. Logical. Even comforting.

But they were wrong.
Spectacularly wrong.

Over the years, I watched company after company reach the same moment, a strange, silent, unsettling point where growth didn't decline dramatically but simply stopped expanding. The company wasn't failing. It wasn't bleeding. It wasn't collapsing. It was just… stuck.

A quiet plateau.
A hesitation point.
A ceiling that no one could see but everyone could feel.

The leaders always said the same thing:
"We're doing everything right. Why isn't it working anymore?"

I could feel their confusion because I had been there myself earlier in my career, the moment when momentum dries up but no one knows why.

Eight-figure companies hit ceilings not because they lack capability, talent, intelligence, or desire. They hit ceilings because architecture has limits. And most leaders only discover those limits at the worst possible moment, when they are already leaning against them.

I once walked into a strategy day for a £32M company where the energy in the room felt heavy despite their financial success. The CEO greeted me with a tired smile, a smile that told me he'd been carrying weight for months without a clear explanation for it. His board sat with the polite stiffness of people pretending everything was fine.

Within minutes, I could sense the ceiling in the room.
It wasn't in the numbers.
It wasn't in the product.
It wasn't in the people.

It was in the architecture.

Eight-figure companies grow through force, talent, speed, instinct, hunger, and momentum. That's how they reach eight figures in the first place. But none of those qualities can take them beyond the ceiling.

Because momentum is not architecture.
Talent is not architecture.
Hard work is not architecture.

The ceiling appears when the internal structure can no longer carry the external ambition.

During that strategy day, as each executive presented their updates, I could feel the same pattern unfolding, a pattern I've seen across continents, industries, cultures, and leadership styles. The company was no longer scaling; it was stretching. And stretched architecture eventually snaps.

Their departments were performing individually, but not collectively. Their decisions were intelligent, but slow. Their managers were strong, but overwhelmed. Their systems were documented, but outdated. Their meetings were frequent, but unproductive. Their growth strategies were ambitious, but inconsistent with what the internal load-bearing structure could sustain.

The CEO kept using the phrase "growing pains."
But growing pains fade.
Ceilings do not.

After hours of listening, I asked one simple question:
"What do you believe is limiting your growth right now?"

Their answers came quickly, too quickly.
Market conditions. Recruitment challenges. Economic turbulence.
Then, almost apologetically, someone blamed the CRM.

None of it was true.
They were naming symptoms.
Not structure.

When I told them, gently, "Your architecture is carrying weight it was never built to carry," the room fell quiet. The kind of quiet that means everyone felt it before they heard it.

The CEO leaned back in his chair and whispered, "I've suspected that, but I didn't know how to explain it."

Most leaders sense the ceiling long before they can articulate it.

The invisible ceiling is not a number, it's a pattern. It appears when:

— decisions escalate instead of distribute
— departments thicken instead of align
— leaders work harder instead of differently
— success becomes heavier instead of easier
— growth requires force instead of flow
— new hires solve nothing
— systems anchor rather than accelerate

It is a structural truth:
Eight figures demand architecture.
Nine figures demand mastery of architecture.

The moment a company crosses the £10M–£30M threshold, instinct stops working. The founder's intuition, once a superpower, becomes a bottleneck. The leadership team, once agile and tightly connected, becomes fragmented under the weight of volume. The processes that worked beautifully at £5M collapse under the complexity of £25M.

One CEO once told me, "It feels like the company is pushing back."
It wasn't pushing back.
It was protecting itself from structural overload.

Growth without architecture is a form of pressure.
And pressure always finds the weakest point.

I remember visiting a manufacturing company near Birmingham that had reached £18M after years of consistent expansion. They were proud, and rightfully so. But the CEO confided something to me during a break in the meeting. He said, "It feels like we're rowing with more people in the boat, but the boat hasn't gotten any bigger."

He was exactly right.
That's what ceilings feel like.

Not crisis. Constraint.

The organisation is trying to scale through effort rather than capacity. And effort cannot lift ceilings; only architecture can.

As I observed their workflow, I saw why growth had slowed. Departments were making decisions independently because the decision architecture had not scaled with the organisation. Communication travelled too slowly because the pathways were built for a smaller, simpler structure. Problems escalated too often because leaders were carrying load instead of distributing it. Their operational system was designed for volume, not complexity. Their talent structure was designed for execution, not replication. Their processes were designed for today, not tomorrow.

Every invisible ceiling has the same cause:
the internal design lags behind the external ambition.

Once the architecture lags, growth stops.
Not because the company lacks ambition, but because the architecture protects itself from collapse.

I told the CEO of that manufacturing company something that changed how he saw scale forever:

"You're not stuck because you lack capability.
You're stuck because you outgrew your architecture faster than you grew your design."

He nodded, almost relieved.
Because once you name the ceiling, it stops being mysterious.
It becomes structural.
And once something becomes structural, it can be redesigned.

Scalability is not about size.
It is about shape.
It is about how weight moves through the organisation, how decisions land, how systems carry the load, how leadership distributes authority, and how the architecture expands without fracturing.

Most companies believe they have hit a ceiling when revenue plateaus.
But ceilings appear long before numbers reveal them.
They appear in meetings.
In hesitations.
In delays.
In tension.
In the silent exhaustion of good people.

Eight-figure companies do not fail at growth.
They fail at architecture.

And the moment a leader finally understands that truth, the ceiling stops being the limit.
It becomes the invitation.

Growth Is Not Scale

There is a moment in almost every boardroom I've ever entered where a leader uses the words "growth" and "scale" interchangeably. They say them as if they are siblings, sometimes even twins. But they are not siblings. They are not cousins. They are not even distant relatives.

Growth and scale are entirely different species, born from different architectures, driven by different energies, and sustained by different truths.

Growth is additive.
Scale is multiplicative.

Growth consumes.
Scale liberates.

Growth increases complexity.
Scale simplifies it.

Growth demands effort.
Scale demands architecture.

But most leaders never see the difference until the company begins to strain under the weight of its own success.

I once sat across from a CEO in the heart of London, a man whose company had crossed £50M in revenue and was celebrated as one of the fastest-growing firms in his industry. His team described him as visionary, relentless, and intensely committed. And he was all of those things. But sitting in that boardroom, surrounded by charts showing impressive revenue curves, he looked... tired.

Not physically.
Architecturally.

He leaned forward, rubbing his forehead, and said quietly, "We're growing faster than ever, but it feels harder every quarter. I thought growth was supposed to get easier."

I smiled gently. "It gets easier when you scale," I said. "But you've been growing, not scaling."

He looked genuinely confused.
No one had ever explained the difference to him.

So I gave him the explanation I've shared with leaders from London to Dubai, New York to Singapore, the explanation that almost always triggers the same stunned silence.

"Growth is when your organisation produces more because your people work harder," I said. "Scale is when your organisation produces more because your architecture works smarter."

He sat back, absorbing it.

Then I added the line that completed the picture:
"You are succeeding through force, not design."

Growth is force.
Scale is design.

He nodded slowly.
He finally understood why his success felt heavy.

The Hidden Cost of Growth

Growth seduces leaders because it feels exciting.
It feels alive.
It feels like proof.

Revenue rises.
Headcount rises.
Clients rise.
Demand rises.
Activity rises.

It feels like progress because everything is expanding.

But growth has a hidden cost:
Everything you add adds weight.

More people means more decisions.
More clients means more complexity.
More revenue means more pressure.
More opportunity means more coordination.

Growth increases everything, not just the things you want more of.

I once watched a technology company grow from £8M to £22M in less than two years. The founder proudly celebrated each milestone. But behind the scenes, the company was exhausting itself. Every new revenue breakthrough created new fires. Every new hire created new confusion. Every new client created new strain.

They weren't scaling.
They were inflating.

Growth makes organisations bigger.
Scale makes them stronger.

There is a difference, an expensive one.

What Scale Actually Is

Scale is not more.
Scale is more with less friction.

It is architecture working in your favour.
It is systems carrying the load instead of people.
It is clarity replacing chaos.
It is flow replacing force.
It is alignment replacing heroics.

Scale is when the organisation begins to multiply its output without multiplying its exhaustion.
When the work becomes lighter as the company becomes heavier.

Most leaders never experience this feeling.
But when they do, they never forget it.

One CEO once described scale to me like this:
"It feels like the company finally started running with me instead of making me drag it."

That is scale.
It is a structural phenomenon.
Not a financial one.

A Short Example: Growth vs Scale

Here is the story I told the London CEO, a simple example he never forgot.

A retail company in Manchester decided to "scale" because demand was rising. They hired more staff. They added more managers. They opened more stores. They extended their product lines. Their revenue doubled in eighteen months.

But costs grew faster than profits.
Turnover increased.
Decision-making slowed.
Quality dipped.
The founder became the bottleneck for everything.

They believed they had scaled.
They had grown.

Now compare that to a logistics company I once advised in Birmingham. Instead of hiring more people, they redesigned their systems. They mapped decisions. They automated handoffs. They simplified communication pathways. They clarified accountability. They rebuilt their workflows around flow, not effort.

Six months later, with the **same team**, they handled **4×** the volume.

They didn't add weight.
They removed friction.

That is the difference between growth and scale.

One company added more people and became heavier.
The other redesigned architecture and became faster.

One grew.
One scaled.

Why Leaders Confuse the Two

Leaders confuse growth with scale for one simple reason:
Growth makes noise.
Scale makes silence.

Growth is loud, new hires, new offices, new activities, new products.
Scale is quiet, fewer decisions, fewer bottlenecks, fewer crises.

Growth feels exciting.
Scale feels calm.

And leaders, especially founders, are conditioned to associate excitement with success.

But the moment a company hits eight figures, excitement becomes the enemy. It creates tension, not traction. The company no longer needs adrenaline. It needs architecture. It no longer needs more people. It needs more clarity. It no longer needs hustle. It needs pathways.

When I tell leaders this, they often look at me as though I've just told them the world is round.
They nod slowly, blinking, as if something old has suddenly dissolved.

Because deep down, they know the truth:
Their growth is heavy.
They don't want it to be.
But they don't know another way.

That's why they hit ceilings.
And that's why scale remains a mystery.

The Emotional Trap of Growth

I've seen leaders fight desperately to expand because they fear slowing down. They push their teams. They expand product lines. They push into new markets. They widen their target audience. They take on more work than they should.

They use pressure as propulsion.
But pressure only works until the structure cracks.

Growth can be addictive, because the numbers tell a seductive story.
But the numbers never reveal the internal cost, the exhaustion, the drift, the bottlenecks, the lost alignment, the people who stay late because the architecture refuses to carry what it should.

Scale, on the other hand, is almost boring to watch.

Everything becomes predictable.
Workflows become fluid.
Teams become lighter.
Leaders breathe again.

There is no chaos.
No adrenaline.
No drama.
Just flow.

And leaders often resist flow because they mistake calm for complacency.

But calm is not complacency.
Calm is structural intelligence.

When Growth Becomes Dangerous

Growth becomes dangerous when leaders assume they can think their way out of structural constraints. They try to solve ceilings with energy instead of design. They push harder instead of pausing. They add more instead of removing friction.

Eight-figure companies rarely collapse because the market turns.
They collapse because they outrun their architecture.

I once told a CEO, "Your company is not failing. It is protecting itself from you."
He didn't like it.
But he understood it.

Growth will take you to eight figures.
But growth will never take you beyond eight figures.

The transition into true scale requires a structural shift, a shift from instinct to architecture, from force to flow, from acceleration to alignment, from leadership heroics to leadership design.

The Structural Truth Leaders Must Accept

After four decades of watching companies rise, stall, and rise again, the truth has become clear:

Growth is the first mountain.
Scale is the second.

Most leaders spend their entire careers climbing the first, never realising the second is where their legacy is built.

Growth shows you what your organisation can do.
Scale shows you what your organisation can become.

Growth is a sprint.
Scale is architecture.

Growth is impressive.
Scale is inevitable, when designed correctly.

And once you feel the difference, once you taste what scale actually feels like, there is no going back. Because scale isn't simply more.
Scale is *more with less weight*.

Why Your Vehicle Determines What Can Scale

The first time I realised that a company's ability to scale had almost nothing to do with its ambition, and everything to do with its Vehicle, I was standing in a warehouse in the outskirts of Birmingham. The CEO, a man with infinite energy and even greater optimism, walked me through the operation with a proud smile, pointing at machines, people, systems, and dashboards as if each held the secret of his next breakthrough.

He kept saying the same phrase:
"We just need to scale this."

But every time he said "this," he pointed at something different.
A machine.
A department.
A process.
A product line.
A new initiative.

He wasn't pointing at a Vehicle.
He was pointing at pieces.

And pieces do not scale.
Vehicles scale.

We ended the tour in his office, where he sat down heavily and said, "Moe, we're pushing so hard. We're expanding into new markets. We're hiring aggressively. We're increasing production. But the more we try to scale, the slower everything becomes."

I looked at him, then said the sentence that changed the entire conversation:

"You're not scaling your company.
 You're dragging your Vehicle."

He frowned. "What do you mean?"

So I told him the truth no one had told him:

"You're trying to scale outputs without redesigning the engine that produces them."

What a Vehicle Actually Is

Most leaders think their Vehicle is their product, service, or business model. But your Vehicle is far more than that.

Your Vehicle is the *entire mechanism* through which you deliver your Value to the market. It is the structural container that determines:

- how fast you can grow

- how heavy the organisation can become

- how many customers you can serve

- how much friction the system can absorb

- how many decisions can move through the structure

- how much complexity the organisation can carry

Your Vehicle is the architecture that either multiplies your ambition or suffocates it.

Some Vehicles scale beautifully, with fluidity, speed, and predictability. Others break the moment pressure increases.

And here is the truth that most leaders do not realise until it's too late:

You cannot scale a Vehicle designed for craftsmanship.
You cannot scale a Vehicle built on heroics.
You cannot scale a Vehicle reliant on memory.

You cannot scale a Vehicle that requires your presence.

You can only scale a Vehicle designed for replication and flow.

Anything else collapses under the weight of growth.

The Misalignment That Kills Scale

Back in that Birmingham warehouse, the company believed they had a
growth problem.
They didn't.
They had a Vehicle problem.

Their business model required customisation.
Their delivery required manual intervention.
Their system required tribal knowledge.
Their decision-making required escalation.
Their operations required improvisation.

None of these are wrong.
But none of these scale.

As he talked proudly about "rolling this out nationwide," I felt a heaviness
move through me, the intuition that comes from four decades of watching
companies unknowingly outrun their own Vehicles.

I asked him quietly, "What part of this model replicates without you?"

He looked around the warehouse.
He looked at his people.
He looked at me.
Then he whispered, "Nothing."

And that was the truth.

He didn't have a scalable Vehicle.
He had a successful one, but successful and scalable are not synonyms.

Success can be carried by talent.
Scale must be carried by architecture.

The Dubai Company That Scaled the Wrong Thing

In Dubai, I once advised a company whose founders believed they were scaling beautifully. They were expanding into new markets, adding new product lines, and chasing opportunity after opportunity. Revenue looked impressive, at first.

But something strange was happening beneath the surface.
Their cost base exploded.
Their complexity multiplied.
Their leadership bandwidth evaporated.
Their decision load became unbearable.
Their operational rhythm fractured under pressure.

They came to me for "growth strategy."

But what they needed was Vehicle surgery.

The core issue was simple: their Vehicle required intimacy. Their strength had always been deep relationships, customised delivery, and founder-driven trust. That model works exquisitely at early-stage and even early eight-figure levels. But it cannot scale geographically, operationally, or structurally.

They had attempted to scale a relationship-driven Vehicle into a volume-driven market.
A fatal mismatch.

It took months of work, and even more courage, for them to admit the truth:

It's not that we can't scale.
It's that we were scaling the wrong thing."

When they redesigned the Vehicle, repositioning the business around repeatability rather than intimacy, everything changed. The same team, the same product, the same leadership.
But a different Vehicle.
And suddenly, scale became possible.

Vehicles shape destinies.
No amount of ambition can compensate for Vehicle misalignment.

The Moment a Vehicle Reveals Itself

Every Vehicle reveals its natural limits long before the numbers show strain. If you watch closely, you will see the signs:

— meetings grow heavier, not lighter
— decisions require more force
— people begin protecting the system instead of improving it
— success feels harder, not easier
— growth increases chaos instead of reducing it

These are not motivational issues.
These are Vehicle issues.

Your Vehicle is silently telling you, "I cannot carry this weight."

Leaders often interpret these signals emotionally.
They push harder.
They work longer.
They hire more.
They expand faster.

But you cannot outwork a misdesigned Vehicle.
You can only redesign it.

A Vehicle Built on You Will Collapse on You

There is one truth leaders hate hearing but desperately need:

If your Vehicle depends on you, your organisation cannot scale beyond you.

For years, I watched founders unknowingly trap their companies inside their own brilliance.
Their intuition made early growth possible.
Their decisions made speed possible.
Their personality made culture possible.
Their presence made success possible.

But that same presence becomes the ceiling.

You cannot scale personal excellence.
You can only scale architectural excellence.

Your Vehicle must eventually replace you, not emotionally, but structurally.

When founders hear this, some look relieved.
Others look terrified.

But all of them know it's true.

The Power of Choosing the Right Vehicle

The strongest companies I've worked with didn't scale because they had the best product or the best people. They scaled because they chose the right Vehicle, the model that could carry their Value repeatedly, predictably, and elegantly.

When your Vehicle is aligned with your Value, your systems become lighter.
When your Vehicle is aligned with your Vision, your growth becomes directional.
When your Vehicle is aligned with your architecture, scale becomes inevitable.

The Vehicle determines the following long before you realise it:

- the talent you hire

- the decisions you centralise or distribute

- the friction your business can absorb

- the systems you need to build

- the speed at which you can grow

- the markets you can enter

- the customers you can serve

- the plateau you will hit

Every success you have, and every ceiling you hit, comes back to this truth:

Your Vehicle is the architecture of your future.
Not your ambition.
Not your effort.
Your Vehicle.

The Conversation That Always Changes Leaders

When I sit with eight-figure CEOs who feel stuck, overwhelmed, or mysteriously constrained, I ask a single question:

"What exactly are you trying to scale, the organisation or the Vehicle that drives it?"

Most of them fall silent.
Because they've never separated the two.

But once they do, the fog lifts.
The ceiling lowers.
The architecture becomes visible.

And they finally see why growth once felt exhilarating, but scale now feels impossible:

They were trying to scale inside the wrong Vehicle.

My Biggest Scaling Misdiagnosis

There are moments in a career when you realise hindsight has sharper vision than you ever did. Moments where you look back and see yourself clearly, not as the Strategic Architect you are today, but as the man who still believed effort could compensate for structure, or that intelligence could outrun design, or that instinct was enough to carry weight that only architecture could hold.

One of those moments came with a company I advised more than fifteen years ago, a company I misdiagnosed so profoundly that the lesson still echoes inside me today. Not because they suffered alone, but because my misreading made their journey harder than it needed to be.

The company was a fast-growing services firm based in the North of England, hovering around the £20M mark, and poised, or so I thought, to break through into the next tier. They had a charismatic founder, a loyal team, a strong brand presence, and an energy that filled every room they walked into.

And like so many leaders at that stage, they were convinced something external was holding them back.

"We should be bigger," the founder told me during our first meeting. "We're better than our competitors. We're smarter. We work harder. There's no reason we can't double over the next eighteen months."

He believed the ceiling they were hitting was marketing-related. Or sales-related. Or competitor-related. Or product-related. Every month the explanation changed, but the urgency remained the same.

I believed him.

That was my mistake.

Their problem wasn't external.
It was internal.
It was structural.
It was architectural.
And I didn't see it early enough.

The False Assumption That Blinded Me

I had been seduced by their momentum.
Their numbers looked strong.
Their culture felt alive.
Their meetings were fast-paced, full of energy and possibility.
Their people were committed in a way you rarely see at that scale.

I assumed, wrongly, that this meant the architecture was strong.

This is the trap that catches even experienced advisors: mistaking enthusiasm for capability, mistaking speed for clarity, mistaking ambition for design.

I thought they had a visibility issue.
What they really had was a Vehicle issue.

But because I misdiagnosed the problem, I made recommendations that pulled them in the wrong direction, strategies that made them faster, not stronger. Strategies that expanded volume without expanding load-bearing capacity.

I helped them grow.
But I did not help them scale.

And the difference became painfully clear months later.

The First Sign I Missed

The first crack appeared when they expanded into a second region. The launch looked impressive, well-staffed, well-funded, well-planned. But within weeks, operational friction emerged everywhere. Internal communication slowed. Processes became inconsistent. The leadership team became stretched and irritable. Decision-making stalled.

At the time, I misdiagnosed this as a "leadership bandwidth issue." I believed they simply needed more managers to absorb the complexity.

That was wrong.
They didn't have a bandwidth issue.
They had a Vehicle that couldn't replicate.

You cannot scale a model that depends on proximity, memory, and founder intuition.
I knew this.
But I ignored the signs.

And because of that misdiagnosis, I recommended structural hires that were unnecessary and expensive. People who entered an environment they could not stabilise. People who drowned quietly inside an architecture that could not carry them.

The founder trusted me.
And my advice added weight instead of removing it.

That truth still stings.

The Day the Ceiling Revealed Itself

The turning point came during a quarterly strategy review. We were in a modern conference room overlooking the city. The founder paced the floor, agitated. His leadership team sat around the table, all of them exhausted in a way that wasn't physical, it was architectural.

"It doesn't make sense," he said. "We're doing everything we're supposed to do. We've invested in sales. We've invested in marketing. We've invested in people. We've invested in systems. Why aren't we breaking through the ceiling?"

I looked around the room and finally saw what I had been refusing to see.

The ceiling wasn't external.
The ceiling was the Vehicle.
The very model they were trying to scale was the thing that prevented scale.

139

Their process required constant escalation.
Their delivery required local nuance.
Their product required customisation.
Their people absorbed complexity instead of processing it.
Their systems supported volume, not replication.

Everything about their Vehicle screamed:
"We can grow.
But we cannot scale."

At that moment, the realisation hit me with a quiet force:
I had misdiagnosed the problem from day one.

I had believed the founder's story instead of reading the architecture.
I had accepted their narrative instead of questioning the Vehicle.
I had assumed momentum equalled scalability when, in truth, momentum often hides structural fragility.

And the cost of that misdiagnosis had been real, financially, operationally, and emotionally.

The Conversation That Still Lives Inside Me

After the meeting, I asked the founder to step outside with me. We stood in the hallway, overlooking a busy street below. The weight in his posture was unmistakable.

"Moe," he said, "I feel like I've lost control of the company."

"You haven't lost control," I replied softly. "You've reached the limit of your Vehicle."

He stared at me, confused.
So I continued.

"You built a model designed for craftsmanship. You're trying to scale it like a factory. That's why it's breaking. You're forcing an identity that doesn't match the architecture."

He went silent.

Then he said something I've never forgotten:

"I thought scale meant doing more.
I didn't realise it meant doing differently."

His voice cracked on the word "differently."
Not from weakness, from truth landing harder than expected.

I took a deep breath.
There are moments where honesty feels like surgery, necessary, painful, and precise.

"I should have seen this sooner," I told him. "I misdiagnosed the problem. And because of that, I helped you push harder when we should have redesigned. I focused on speed when I should have focused on structure."

He didn't say anything for a long time.
Then he nodded.
Not in blame, but in recognition.

Leaders forgive you when you tell them the truth.
What they cannot forgive is avoidance.

The Turning Point That Followed

For the next six months, we rebuilt the company from the inside out. We simplified their delivery model. We redefined roles. We redesigned processes for replication instead of improvisation. We rebuilt decision pathways. We clarified their Value proposition. And, most importantly, we redesigned the Vehicle, the operational engine that actually creates scale.

Only then did growth become lift instead of drag.
Only then did decisions speed up.
Only then did the organisation regain energy.
Only then did the ceiling finally lower.

They didn't double in eighteen months, as originally planned.
But they did something far more important:

They became scalable.

Growth is impressive.
Scale is transformative.

But scale only begins when the Vehicle is redesigned for it.

The Lesson That Changed My Work Forever

My misdiagnosis taught me one truth I now carry into every boardroom, every WarRoom, every private session:

You cannot solve a scaling problem with growth solutions.

More people will not fix it.
More systems will not fix it.
More marketing will not fix it.
More opportunity will not fix it.

Only architecture will.

And architecture begins with one question that I now ask much earlier:

"What exactly are you trying to scale, the model you have, or the model you wish you had?"

Most leaders grow the model they have.
Few scale the model they need.

This misdiagnosis taught me to see the difference instantly.
It sharpened my instincts.
It humbled my approach.
It made me better.

Because some lessons come from strategy.
Others come from scars.

This one came from both.

The Courage to Stop Scaling Bad Structure

There is a moment in every leader's journey where the bravest decision is not to accelerate, but to stop. Not because momentum has disappeared, and not because the company has failed, but because something deeper inside the architecture is quietly warning:
"If you keep pushing, this will break."

Stopping is one of the most difficult decisions a leader can make.
Not because they lack intelligence.
Not because they lack ambition.
But because they have spent their entire lives equating forward motion with progress.

I have sat in countless boardrooms where everyone could feel something was wrong, yet no one dared to name it. The charts on the screen told a confident story. The team spoke with conviction. The founder tried to radiate certainty. But beneath the surface, the structure was already cracking.

It takes courage to look at a growing company, a company praised by the market, envied by competitors, admired by its peers, and admit that the internal scaffolding cannot carry the next chapter. Most leaders only stop when they are forced to. The strongest ones stop before the collapse.

I remember working with a £40M organisation in London that had been expanding aggressively for three consecutive years. They had moved into new markets, launched new product lines, and absorbed two acquisitions. Revenue looked extraordinary. The board felt triumphant. Investors were celebrating.

But I could feel something else.

Their meetings were heavier.
Decisions took longer.
Handoffs grew fuzzy.
The leadership team looked drained in a way that numbers cannot reveal.

One afternoon, after a board meeting that felt more like a rescue operation than a strategic discussion, I asked the CEO to stay behind. He closed the door gently and sank into the chair across from me.

"Moe," he said, "everyone expects us to keep pushing. But I feel like the company is leaning so far forward that one wrong step will tip us over."

His voice wasn't fearful.
It was honest.

I told him something few leaders ever hear at that stage of growth:
"You don't need to push harder.
You need to stop, and redesign."

He looked stunned.
Not offended, relieved.

Leaders often carry the quiet fear that pausing looks weak.
But pausing is structural wisdom.

I explained what I could see clearly:
"You're scaling bad structure. You're adding weight to a design that wasn't engineered for it. Every new initiative is landing on weak foundations. If you continue, the organisation won't just stall, it will snap."

He exhaled deeply, the kind of breath that releases months of tension.

"What do we do?" he asked.

"We stop," I replied. "Not permanently. Just long enough to rebuild the load paths."

Stopping doesn't mean retreat.
Stopping means choosing design over disaster.

We paused all expansion initiatives for ninety days.
No new market entries.
No product launches.
No acquisitions.
No major system changes.

Instead, we rebuilt the architecture.

We clarified the Vehicle.
We realigned the operating rhythm.
We simplified decision pathways.
We removed layers of unnecessary complexity.
We repaired the structural fractures that were previously ignored in the push for more.

And something remarkable happened.

The company didn't lose momentum.
It regained capacity.

Leaders felt lighter.
Teams moved faster.
Communication sharpened.

Systems flowed.
Decisions accelerated.

Stopping gave them strength.
Stopping gave them speed.
Stopping saved them.

The CEO later said something I'll never forget:
"Stopping felt like admitting failure... until I realised it was the first time
in years we were building for the company we wanted, not the company we
inherited."

That sentence captures the essence of architectural leadership.

Because scale is not a celebration of more.
Scale is the discipline of better.

Most companies fail at scale not because they lack opportunity, but because
they lack the courage to pause before adding weight. They keep expanding
because they fear slowing down. They fear being misunderstood. They fear
being judged. They fear the quiet of reflection after years of noise.

But scale rewards the brave, not the busy.

I tell leaders this often:
"You can grow on adrenaline.
You can only scale on architecture."

And architecture cannot be rebuilt at full speed.

There is no shame in pausing.
There is only wisdom in it.

Pausing is how you strengthen the foundation.
Pausing is how you redesign the Vehicle.
Pausing is how you remove friction before adding fuel.
Pausing is how you prevent a collapse.

Real courage isn't accelerating when the world expects it.
Real courage is pausing when your architecture requires it.

The leaders who scale sustainably, the ones who cross £100M, £250M,
£500M, are not the ones who push hardest.
They are the ones who notice the fracture earliest.
They are the ones who choose design over ego.
They are the ones who understand that a pause is not a setback.
It is the moment the future begins.

CHAPTER 7:
Sustainability, The Resilience-Bearing Pillar

What Breaks First Under Pressure

People often assume organisations break at their weakest point, the struggling department, the underperforming leader, the outdated system. It sounds logical, almost comforting, because it suggests that fragility is visible. But organisations rarely break where you expect them to. After four decades inside boardrooms, I've learned that pressure reveals the fracture hidden beneath competence, not beside it.

It breaks where weight accumulates in silence.

One of the earliest moments I recognised this truth was during a crisis inside a £60M firm I was advising in London. On paper, they were unstoppable, rapid growth, strong EBITDA, a respected brand, and a leadership team that looked as if it had been carved from a brochure for high-performance executives. They wore confidence like armour.

Yet something felt wrong the moment I entered the room.

It wasn't the numbers; the numbers were immaculate. It wasn't the team; the team was intelligent and articulate. It wasn't the meeting; the meeting was structured and polished.

It was the silence between the sentences.

You can learn more about an organisation from its pauses than from its presentations.
And that day, the pauses were heavy.

As the CFO walked through quarterly results, the CEO nodded mechanically, his expression tight, his smile rehearsed. The COO scribbled notes faster than anyone could possibly think. The HR director kept glancing at the CEO before she answered anything. It was a choreography of competence masking something far more fragile.

147

Pressure doesn't expose incompetence.
Pressure exposes imbalance.

Halfway through the meeting, it happened. A supply chain disruption, minor in the grand scheme of business, triggered a cascade of disagreements. Voices sharpened. Blame flickered across the table. People defended territories rather than solving problems.

It wasn't the disruption that caused the collapse, it was the structure that had been carrying too much unspoken tension for too long.

After the meeting, the CEO asked to speak privately. We sat in his office, the city's skyline stretching behind him like a reminder of the height he was expected to maintain.

"Moe," he said quietly, "I feel like everything will break if one more thing goes wrong."

"It's already breaking," I replied. "You're just holding the pieces together faster than they can fall apart."

He didn't argue. He didn't pretend. He didn't deflect. For the first time that day, he dropped the armour.

"Where do you think the real problem is?" he asked.

"In the part of your organisation that looks the strongest," I said. "Because that is where you've been placing the most weight."

He leaned back, stunned. "How can the strongest part be the most fragile?"

"Because strength attracts responsibility," I said. "Responsibility attracts pressure. And pressure breaks whatever carries it longest."

He closed his eyes. He knew exactly what I meant.

The Paradox of Organisational Strength

Every company has areas that rise when others fall, high performers, dependable departments, leaders who step in when things become chaotic. They become the safety net, the stabiliser, the invisible backbone.

But pressure doesn't distribute evenly.
It gravitates.

The more reliable someone is, the more load they are asked to carry.
The more competent a team becomes, the more crises are funnelled toward them.
The more stable a department appears, the more decisions are dumped onto it.

People don't break from weakness.
They break from carrying too much weight without structural relief.

The company in London wasn't failing because of its problems.
It was failing because its successes hid the strain beneath.

The Quiet Collapse

A few weeks later, the COO resigned. Not with drama. Not with anger. With exhaustion. She told the CEO she felt like a "shock absorber" for the entire company.

She wasn't wrong.

The structure had been designed, unintentionally, in a way that channelled every unresolved issue through her. People trusted her. She was capable. She was calm. She was clear.

And that is precisely why the architecture broke at her.

The strongest steel snaps hardest when it carries weight it was never designed to hold.

This is the part leaders do not see until it is too late:
Resilience is not about individual strength.
It is about systemic distribution.

When pressure rises, bad structure turns competence into captivity.

The Weight You Don't See

Every organisation has three silent pressure points:

1. **The person who absorbs more decisions than they should.**

2. **The process that no longer fits but no one wants to challenge.**

3. **The cultural expectation that certain people will always "figure it out."**

These fractures don't appear on spreadsheets.
They don't show up in dashboards.
They don't announce themselves in meetings.

But they bend quietly.
And eventually they snap loudly.

I once told a founder, "You're not leading a company. You're managing a slow leak."
He didn't understand what I meant, not until six months later when his most dependable leader walked away, taking twenty years of institutional knowledge with him.

Bad structure breaks good people.

Why Sustainability Begins With Honesty

Sustainability isn't about endurance.
It isn't about toughness.
It isn't about surviving storms.

Sustainability is the architecture that prevents storms from turning into collapses.

It requires honesty, the kind leaders rarely have time for when the company is growing quickly. Honesty about where weight truly lives. Honesty about the decisions that create silent pressure. Honesty about the friction that no one talks about because the numbers look good.

The CEO from the London firm later told me, "The worst part wasn't seeing the cracks. It was realising how long we pretended not to."

That is the price of pressure:
Silence becomes normal.
Strain becomes invisible.
Breaking becomes inevitable.

Unless you redesign the structure *before* you need it.

150

What Breaks First Is Always Predictable

After four decades, I can walk into almost any organisation and identify what will break first under pressure. It is never the department everyone worries about. It is never the manager who struggles. It is never the system that underperforms.

It is always the area that carries the most unexamined weight.
The role that has become too central.
The leader who is too dependable.
The process that everyone relies on but no one questions.
The cultural norm that rewards quiet sacrifice.

Sustainability means redesigning this weight-bearing architecture long before it collapses.

Because pressure does not create fractures.
Pressure reveals them.

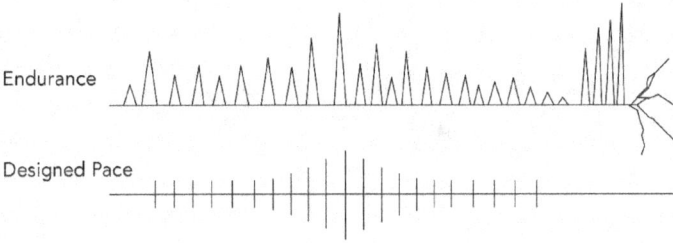

The Drift I Did Not Catch in Time

Every leader believes they will recognise danger when it arrives. They imagine it will come with noise, disruption, tension, conflict, something dramatic enough to command attention. But drift never arrives loudly. Drift arrives quietly. And quiet is far more dangerous than chaos.

I learned this the hard way.

Years ago, I worked with a £25M company in the Midlands that had grown rapidly over a five-year period. They were ambitious, energetic, and fiercely proud of what they had built. The leadership team trusted one another. The culture felt alive. The founder radiated a confidence that suggested nothing could shake them.

But something subtle was shifting beneath the surface, something I sensed, but didn't investigate deeply enough at the time.

Their weekly leadership meetings had changed tone. A few years earlier, those meetings were crisp, aligned, and filled with strategic clarity. Everyone understood the direction. Everyone understood the priorities. Everyone moved with a shared sense of momentum.

But slowly, almost imperceptibly, the clarity began to fade.

Questions that once had sharp answers became vague.
Projects that once moved smoothly began to stall.
Ownership blurred.
Deadlines drifted.
Work carried weight that shouldn't have been there.

It wasn't dysfunction.
It wasn't crisis.
It was drift.

And drift feels harmless, until it isn't.

One afternoon, during a routine review session, I noticed something disturbing. Each leader described their priorities differently. Their goals no longer aligned. Their interpretations of the company's strategy had begun to diverge. It wasn't blatant. Nothing alarming. Just slight variations, the kind you tell yourself can be corrected later.

I remember thinking, *We'll tighten this up next quarter.*

But next quarter was too late.

The First Sign I Ignored

A senior leader, someone highly respected by the team, began making decisions that pulled his division away from the company's core direction. At first, these decisions seemed sensible, intelligent even. He was optimising for efficiency and chasing opportunities he believed were strategic.

But here was the truth I failed to recognise:
He wasn't defying strategy.
He was interpreting drift.

He filled the silence left by fading clarity.

Leaders do not misbehave out of rebellion; they misbehave out of ambiguity.

I should have caught it sooner.

But drift is seductive. It disguises itself as busyness, productivity, progress. It gives the illusion that the company is moving forward when, in reality, it is slowly losing direction.

The Moment Drift Became Damage

The collapse began with a customer incident, something minor, the kind of issue any healthy organisation can absorb. But this time, the response was chaotic. Teams miscommunicated. Leadership disagreed. Accountability blurred.

The founder called me late that evening, his voice tight.

"Moe," he said, "I don't understand what's happening. Everyone is working hard, but everything is falling apart."

I arrived the next morning and reviewed the operations. It didn't take long to see the truth:

The company hadn't failed overnight.
It had been drifting for eighteen months.

Decision-making had stretched.
Departments had started interpreting priorities independently.
Systems remained the same while the business around them changed.
People compensated for unclear direction by protecting their own domain.
Leaders made choices that were technically correct but strategically disconnected.

The drift had been slow, silent, and cumulative, a steady erosion of alignment that created structural fragility.

The customer incident wasn't the cause.
It was the revelation.

The Conversation That Still Haunts Me

The founder and I sat in his office after two exhausting days of assessments. He looked at me with frustration, fear, and something deeper, betrayal, perhaps, though he didn't say it.

"Why didn't you see this earlier?" he asked.

His voice wasn't accusatory.
It was honest.

And he was right to ask.

I took a breath, feeling the weight of my own failure.

"I saw fragments," I said. "But I underestimated the pattern. I mistook drift for noise. I should have intervened sooner."

He nodded slowly, absorbing the words.

Leadership requires courage.
Advisory requires truth.

That day, the truth was painful.

We spent weeks repairing the architecture, realigning teams, rebuilding decision pathways, redesigning the operating rhythm. But repairing drift is harder than preventing drift. Because drift is not a structural problem; it's an identity problem.

And identity takes time to restore.

What Drift Really Is

Drift is not the loss of direction.
It is the quiet accumulation of misalignments.

Drift is when priorities remain unspoken.
Drift is when success hides structural decay.
Drift is when people begin solving the wrong problems beautifully.
Drift is when decisions no longer point in the same direction.
Drift is when leaders are busy instead of coordinated.

Drift does not feel dangerous.
Drift feels familiar.

But familiarity is the enemy of sustainability.

The company survived, but they never regained the pace they once had. Something had fundamentally shifted. The architecture held, but the cultural scar remained.

I still think about them often.
Not with regret, with responsibility.

Because that experience reshaped how I work with every organisation that followed.

The Lesson That Redefined My Craft

Today, when I enter a boardroom, I listen for drift long before I look for failure.

I listen for confusion disguised as confidence.
I listen for politeness replacing alignment.
I listen for decisions that point in parallel, not together.
I listen for leaders who explain rather than execute.
I listen for systems that are followed only when convenient.
I listen for language that sounds similar but means different things to different people.

Drift begins with soft edges.
Sustainability requires sharp ones.

The company taught me something I will never forget:

You cannot catch drift by watching performance.
You can only catch it by watching behaviour.

Because numbers reveal outcomes.
Drift reveals direction.

And direction determines whether a company survives pressure or collapses under it.

How 3XV Protects Long-Term Integrity

If you stay in this work long enough, you realise something that most leaders never see until it is almost too late:
An organisation does not remain healthy because it is brilliant.
It remains healthy because it stays itself.

Integrity, true organisational integrity, is not a moral concept.
It is the structural alignment between who you say you are, what you deliver, and how you operate under pressure.

3XV is the framework that protects that integrity.

I didn't understand this fully until I witnessed a company lose itself.

Years ago, I advised a business in the Midlands that had grown from £5M to nearly £40M in a short span. They were admired in their industry. They were confident, organised, and outwardly successful. Their leadership team spoke with such conviction about their future that even I felt the pull of their ambition.

But ambition has a shadow.
And the shadow appears when identity becomes negotiable.

Their Vision had been clear from the beginning, to dominate a very specific niche. Their Value was precise, a quality of service no competitor could match. Their Vehicle was built to deliver depth, not breadth.

This coherence made them unstoppable in the early years.

But success is a seductive enemy. As opportunities increased, so did their appetite. They chased adjacent markets. They pursued partnerships that diluted their strengths. They launched products their architecture wasn't designed for. They started behaving like a company they were not.

This is how drift begins at the top.
A misaligned decision here.
A convenient opportunity there.
A blurred priority that no one challenges.

At first, the effects were subtle.
But identity decay always begins subtly.

The Moment I Realised Integrity Had Slipped

One morning, during a senior leadership workshop, I asked a simple question:

"What business are you *not* in?"

The room froze.

A few years earlier, every leader would have answered in unison.
But now, one said, "We could expand into X."
Another said, "We should consider Y."
A third said, "Z might be the next big move."

Their answers contradicted each other, and, more importantly, contradicted who they were.

That's when I realised something had fractured:
Their Vision had drifted.
Their Value had diluted.
Their Vehicle had mutated.

They were growing, but they were losing integrity.

Not ethical integrity, architectural integrity.

An organisation loses integrity when identity becomes optional.

3XV is the guardrail that prevents this.

Vision Protects Direction

Vision is not a slogan.
Vision is not a poster.
Vision is not a paragraph written during a strategy day.

Vision is the decision boundary that determines what the company will not become, even when opportunity tries to seduce it.

When Vision is clear, decisions accelerate because the organisation knows where it is going, and where it refuses to go.

When Vision is unclear, the organisation can be pulled in ten different directions at once.
All of them attractive.
None of them aligned.

The Midlands company had a Vision, but they stopped using it. They made decisions on appetite, not architecture. And appetite is never sustainable.

Vision is the compass that protects long-term identity.

3XV restores that compass when it starts to slip.

Value Protects Behaviour

Value is not what you sell.
It is the reason a customer chooses *you* instead of anyone else.

When Value is clear, the organisation behaves consistently.
Teams know what matters.
Leaders know what excellence looks like.
The company knows what to protect and what to ignore.

But when Value drifts, behaviour drifts with it.

In the Midlands company, Value had once been unmistakable, depth, precision, reliability. But as they expanded into markets where these qualities weren't essential, teams began to compromise. They rushed work. They lowered standards. They celebrated speed at the expense of mastery.

Nothing dramatic.
Just subtle erosion.

3XV would have surfaced this instantly.
Because once Value is anchored in the identity, any behaviour that contradicts it becomes visible, and correctable.

Value is the behavioural architecture of sustainability.

Vehicle Protects Capacity

Vision gives direction.
Value gives identity.
Vehicle gives capability.

Your Vehicle determines what the organisation can carry over time, the weight, complexity, decision volume, customer demands, and structural load the business can absorb.

When Vehicle remains aligned with Vision and Value, the organisation stays balanced.
When the Vehicle mutates faster than identity, collapse begins.

This happened in the Midlands company.
Their Vehicle evolved into something their architecture was never designed for.

They became stretched, overextended, and structurally confused.

The irony is that they believed they were scaling.
They weren't.

158

They were shape-shifting.

Scale comes from consistency.
Shape-shifting comes from insecurity.

3XV protects against both.

The Hard Conversation That Followed

I sat with the founder one evening, long after the leadership team had left.
The office was quiet. The glow of the city reflected against the window
behind him. He looked tired, not from work, but from carrying decisions
that had drifted too far from the original identity he once held with absolute
conviction.

"Moe," he said softly, "I don't recognise the company anymore."

"You do," I replied. "You just don't recognise what it's becoming."

He looked at me, waiting.

"You've allowed the company to chase opportunity faster than it could hold
integrity. You didn't lose your way, you lost your anchor."

He nodded, slowly, painfully.

"What do we do?"

"We go back to the identity," I said. "We rebuild 3XV."

We spent months stripping away complexity, removing misaligned initiatives,
consolidating product lines, and re-anchoring the company to what had made
it exceptional in the first place.

And the transformation was immediate.

Not because the company became stronger.
But because it became itself again.

That is the power of 3XV.

3XV Is Not a Strategy Tool. It Is an Integrity System.

3XV ensures:

The Vision remains uncompromised.
The Value remains sacred.
The Vehicle remains aligned.

And when these three remain intact, sustainability is no longer a hope, it becomes inevitability.

Companies do not collapse because they are weak.
They collapse because they forget who they are.

3XV protects the memory.
It protects the identity.
It protects the architecture.

It protects the truth that allows an organisation to survive pressure, endure change, and grow without losing itself.

Because long-term integrity is not maintained through discipline.
It is maintained through design.

And 3XV is the design.

Cultural Architecture and the Cost of Ignoring Truth

Culture is not morale.
Culture is not personality.
Culture is not how people feel on a good day or how they behave at an offsite.

Culture is architecture.

It is the quiet arrangement of truths your organisation is willing to face, and the lies it chooses to tolerate. It is the structure that determines which voices are amplified, which are silenced, and which disappear because speaking up costs more than staying quiet.

I learned the cost of ignoring truth long before I understood the language of architecture. Years ago, when I was still young in this work, I used to get fired for telling the truth. Twenty-seven times in total. Sometimes it took months, sometimes weeks. In one dramatic case, I was fired on the same day I was hired.

The irony is that they all hired me back later. Twenty-two of them within three years.
Not because I changed…
but because their architecture failed exactly where I told them it would.

Truth is the one asset every organisation claims to value but structurally resists when it threatens comfort.

And culture is the system that decides whether truth survives.

The Company That Hid Its Own Reality

Years ago, I worked with a £70M company whose culture was famously "positive." People were polite. Meetings were smooth. The leadership team spoke in polished sentences that could have been rehearsed. They celebrated wins publicly and buried problems privately.

The CEO once told me, "People don't argue here. We're aligned."

But alignment without tension is not alignment. It is suppression.

One morning during a leadership session, I noticed something unsettling. Every time someone mentioned a small operational issue, the CEO would smile and say, "Let's not get stuck in the weeds." He meant well, but his reaction created an unspoken rule:

No bad news in the presence of the boss.

This is how cultural drift begins.
Not through conflict, through avoidance.

The team learned quickly. Problems were diluted before being reported. Risks were softened. Numbers were interpreted generously. Truth became a negotiation.

And the architecture began to distort.

When Culture Punishes Truth, Structure Breaks

A mid-level manager approached me privately one afternoon and said, "Moe… I can show you where the real issues are. But if I speak up in the room, I'll disappear."

He wasn't being dramatic.
He was describing the cultural architecture perfectly.

When the truth costs more than silence, organisations suffocate quietly.

He showed me a series of operational fractures:
Misaligned workflows, outdated systems, hidden communication gaps.
Nothing catastrophic, yet.
But enough to destabilise the entire company over time.

I brought these findings to the CEO in a private meeting. His response was polite, appreciative… and dismissive.

"Moe, I hear you. But we're doing well. Let's stay focused on the big picture."

That sentence is the anthem of companies headed toward architectural collapse.

When leaders ignore micro-truths, they create macro-failures.

The Collapse They Didn't See Coming

Six months later, a major client threatened to leave after a chain of operational errors. These errors weren't new. They were simply the inevitable consequence of the truths they had been avoiding.

The CEO called me late at night. His voice sounded different, stripped of confidence, almost fragile.

"Why didn't I see this?" he asked.

"You did," I answered gently. "You just didn't let the truth land."

Culture determines what truths the architecture accepts.

And architecture determines what pressure the company can endure.

He went silent for a long moment.

"I created a place where people were afraid to speak," he said.

"No," I replied. "You created a place where people had to choose between truth and safety."

It was never about fear.
It was about cost.

The Light Echo of the '27 Firings'

When I was younger, companies fired me because I said things they weren't ready to hear. Not because I was reckless, but because I refused to be complicit in cultures that punished truth.

Back then, I thought it was a personal flaw.
Now I realise it was architectural.

Those leaders weren't firing me.
They were firing the truth.

And when the truth eventually arrived, as it always does, they rehired me, hoping I could repair what had already cracked.

The problem wasn't my message.
The problem was their culture's inability to hold it.

Culture is the load-bearing structure for truth.

If the culture cannot support truth, the architecture cannot support growth.

How 3XV Shapes Cultural Integrity

Vision protects direction.
Value protects behaviour.
Vehicle protects capability.

But culture protects truth.

And truth protects sustainability.

When 3XV is strong, the culture becomes a place where clarity is not punished, misalignment is not ignored, and honesty is not a career risk.

Vision defines the truth the organisation must honour.
Value defines the truth customers expect.
Vehicle defines the truth the architecture can realistically deliver.

Culture is where all three collide.

If the culture bends, everything bends.
If the culture fractures, everything fractures.
If the culture silences truth, the architecture quietly dies.

Sustainable companies are not the ones that avoid failure.
They're the ones designed to expose truth before failure arrives.

The Structural Truth Leaders Must Accept

There is no such thing as a "positive" culture if truth cannot survive inside it.

A healthy culture is not always pleasant.
But it is always honest.

A healthy culture does not protect feelings.
It protects clarity.

A healthy culture does not silence problems.
It surfaces them early enough to prevent collapse.

The companies that scale sustainably, the ones that survive pressure, volatility, growth, and time, are the ones that design cultural architecture deliberately.

And the first design principle is simple:
Truth must cost nothing.

Everything else becomes possible when truth is free.

CHAPTER 8:
Sellability, The Transfer-Bearing Pillar

Every Business Is for Sale, Even When You Do Not Plan to Sell

When I first began advising leaders, I used to believe them when they said, "Moe, I'm never selling this company." They said it with conviction, sometimes with pride, sometimes with the emotional weight of someone who had built their business the way a parent raises a child.

They believed the business was theirs forever.
They believed legacy meant ownership.
They believed selling was a kind of betrayal.

And for years, I didn't challenge them.

But time has a way of revealing truths that comfort cannot hold.
After four decades inside boardrooms, I've learned one thing with absolute certainty:

Every business is for sale, even when you do not plan to sell.

Because the moment you are unable to run it, unwilling to run it, or unfit to run it, the business will sell itself, either intentionally or through deterioration.

Sellability is not a transaction.
Sellability is structural readiness.

It is the architecture of transfer, continuity, independence, and resilience.

A business designed to be sellable is a business designed to survive you.

And that is the moment leaders finally understand this pillar, when they realise sellability has nothing to do with selling, and everything to do with sovereignty.

The First Time This Truth Hit Me

I once worked with a founder whose company was thriving, £28M in revenue, expanding rapidly, adored by their clients. He was one of the most dedicated leaders I'd ever met. He said the same sentence many founders say:

"This business is my life. I'll never sell it."

And then, one ordinary Tuesday, life intervened.

A health incident, sudden, unexpected, non-negotiable, forced him out of the business for six months. No warning. No transition. No preparation. The leadership team panicked. Decisions piled up. Clients became anxious. The bank got nervous. The board began quietly discussing contingency plans.

He didn't sell the business.
The business sold him.

Without him, it collapsed into uncertainty. The architecture had never been designed for independence. It relied on his memory, his relationships, his approvals, his presence. And when he was no longer there to carry the weight, the structure bent.

I sat with him months later as he recovered. He looked at me with the kind of honesty that only comes after life shakes your certainty.

"I thought building a company meant securing my future," he said. "I never realised sellability *is* the future."

That sentence has stayed with me ever since.

Sellability Is Not an Exit Strategy — It's an Operating Philosophy

A sellable business is not built for a buyer.
It is built for continuity.

A sellable business does not need you.
It respects you, but it does not collapse in your absence.

A sellable business is not dependent on relationships that only the founder holds.
It is architected so that trust is replicated, not concentrated.

A sellable business does not rely on heroics.
It relies on systems.

And a sellable business is not a vanity project.
It is an asset, portable, transferable, and structurally independent.

Leaders often flinch when they hear this because it challenges the identity they've built around their companies. But the truth is quietly liberating:

Sellability means freedom.
Freedom for you.
Freedom for the business.
Freedom for the future.

The moment a business becomes sellable, it becomes scalable.
The moment it becomes sellable, it becomes sustainable.
The moment it becomes sellable, it becomes transferable, not just to a buyer, but to successors, partners, leadership teams, and the next generation.

Sellability is the ultimate expression of structural maturity.

The Company That Tripled Its Value Without Trying to Sell

Several years ago, I worked with a firm in Leeds that initially hired me to help them scale. Sellability wasn't even on the agenda, they were still years away from considering an exit. But as we rebuilt their architecture, something unexpected happened.

Their valuation rose.
Their risk profile shrank.
Their operational independence increased.
Their systems became replicable.
Their decision-making became distributed.
Their reliance on the founder evaporated.

One evening, during a strategy review, the founder laughed and said, "Moe, we've accidentally made the business unbelievably sellable."

"No," I replied. "You've intentionally made the business structurally sound."

He paused, absorbing the distinction.

"Is this what sellability really is?" he asked.

"Yes," I said. "Sellability is what happens when architecture grows up."

The irony is that companies designed to be sellable rarely sell.
They don't need to.
Their value compounds without the founder sacrificing life, health, or identity to keep the machine going.

169

Sellability is the architecture of optionality.

Why Leaders Resist the Word 'Sale'

Many founders recoil when they hear the word "sell."
It feels cold.
It feels transactional.
It feels like abandonment.

But that reaction comes from a misunderstanding of what a business really is.

A business is not a child.
A business is not an extension of the founder's ego.
A business is not a monument.

A business is a system of value creation.
A transferable system.
A replicable system.
A living system.

Whether you sell it or not is irrelevant.

What matters is whether the system can continue producing value without you holding every lever.

Sellability is not a decision.
Sellability is a design.

The Architecture of a Sellable Business

When I say, "Every business is for sale," I am not speaking in financial terms. I am speaking architecturally.

Sellability means:

The business can run without your presence.
The business can operate without your memory.
The business can function without your intuition.
The business can grow without your permission.
The business can survive without your protection.

But above all:

The business can be transferred, to anyone, at any time, for any reason.

A sellable business is not vulnerable.
It is durable.

A sellable business is not founder-centric.

170

It is architecture-centric.

A sellable business does not depend on goodwill.
It depends on design.

The Truth Leaders Eventually Accept

You may never list your company.
You may never speak to an investor.
You may never consider an exit.

But one day, someone else will run your business,
either because you choose it…
or because life chooses it for you.

Sellability is preparing for that moment before it arrives.

The founder from the Midlands who once swore he'd never sell eventually passed leadership to his daughter. The transition was smooth, professional, and graceful, not because she was talented, though she was, but because the business had become sellable. The architecture was built for transfer, not protection.

He once told me, "I didn't build a company. I built continuity."

That is the essence of this pillar.

Sellability is the engineering of continuity.
Continuity is the engine of legacy.

And legacy is not what you leave behind,
it is what survives you.

They don't send an email explaining the flaw.
They don't outline the risks they see.
They don't talk about the structural weaknesses behind closed doors.

They simply disappear.

A polite message.
A "change of direction."
A shift in strategy.
A pause in discussions that never resumes.

Founders interpret this as hesitation or negotiation.
It isn't.
It's clarity.

Buyers walk away when they see something the founder cannot yet see:

The business works, but it won't survive the transfer.

This truth is as old as M&A itself, but most owners never learn it until the exit collapses.

I remember a founder in Surrey once telling me, "Moe, they loved the business. They loved the numbers. They loved the product. Why did they vanish?"

I looked him in the eye and said, "Because you were still the business. And they weren't buying *you*."

He didn't speak for a full minute.

That is the moment every founder fears, the moment the truth lands with the weight of a decade:
success built on dependency is not value.
It is liability.

And buyers can smell liability before the founder even senses danger.

Buyers Don't Buy Potential — They Buy Transferability

A strong business impresses a buyer.
A transferable business closes the deal.

Buyers want to know:

Will this company run without the founder's intuition?
Will customers stay when the founder leaves?
Will leaders execute without the founder's approvals?
Will culture remain stable after the transition?
Will decisions continue to flow without the founder present?

If the answer is *no* to even one of these, they will walk.

Not loudly.
Quietly.
Graciously.
Professionally.

Because buyers never want a founder to know the truth that would crush them:

"We love your business.
We just don't believe it can survive you."

The Meeting That Changed My Understanding Forever

Years ago, I was invited to sit in on a buyer's internal review, something advisors rarely get to see. The company for sale was exceptional: £18M revenue, strong profit margins, steady growth, loyal customers. The founder felt confident a deal was within reach.

But in the buyer's room, the mood told a different story.

The CFO went first. "The numbers are solid."
The commercial director added, "Market position is strong."
The operational lead nodded. "Good systems on paper."

Then came the head of risk, a man who spoke carefully and only when absolutely necessary. He opened a folder, paused, and said, "Everything works... but only because the founder is forcing it to work."

He continued, "We're not buying a company. We're buying a man."
Then he closed the folder.

The decision was made in that moment.

The deal died, not because the business was weak, but because the *architecture was personal.*

That founder never knew the real reason.
Buyers never reveal that kind of truth.

They don't want confrontation.
They don't want emotion.
They don't want negotiation.

They want *transferability.*

And if it's missing, they step away silently.

The Hidden Red Flags Buyers See Instantly

Founders believe buyers study numbers.
They do.
But numbers are not what alarms them.

Buyers watch behaviour.
Systems.
Dependencies.
Decision flow.
Role clarity.
Leadership bandwidth.
Organisational load.

One buyer once told me, "We walk away whenever we see a company that works because of heroics."
Heroics may impress customers.
But they terrify buyers.

Heroics signal fragility.
Fragility signals risk.
Risk destroys valuation.

Another buyer said, "If I cannot draw a clean line from customer value → leadership ownership → operational execution, the deal stops."

Founders rarely see these fractures.
Buyers see them immediately.

Buyers look for a team whose conative wiring matches the future load of the business, not the past.

Because if the instinctive energy of the team is misaligned with the weight of the future, the architecture will collapse under pressure long before a buyer signs anything.

The Silent Walk-Away Signals

Over the years, I've learned to recognise the exact moment a buyer loses interest, the moment their body language shifts, their questions soften, their tone changes, their eyes stop looking at the business and start looking at the founder.

The silent walk-away usually begins here:

When the founder answers a question the leadership team should have answered.

When the founder explains a process no one else understands.
When the founder is involved in every major decision.
When customer relationships rely on the founder's reputation.
When culture revolves around the founder's personality.
When product innovation lives inside the founder's head.

The founder sees these moments as demonstrations of commitment.
The buyer sees them as indicators of dependency.

The founder thinks,
"This shows how dedicated I am."

The buyer thinks,
"This shows the business collapses without you."

And when a buyer believes the business collapses when you leave, they will never buy it, at any price.

A Conversation That Every Founder Needs to Hear

I once sat with a founder after a buyer had withdrawn. He looked defeated, confused, and betrayed.

"They told me everything was perfect," he said. "What changed?"

"Nothing changed," I replied. "They simply saw what they needed to see."

"And what was that?"

"That you are the architecture."

He clenched his jaw, not in anger, in recognition.

"No one wants to buy a business they cannot operate," I said gently. "And right now, your business is built inside you. Not outside you."

He lowered his head.
Because he knew I was right.

The hardest truth founders must accept is this:
Buyers don't walk away from businesses.
They walk away from dependency.

They walk away when the company's identity lives inside one person.
They walk away when the systems are fragile.
They walk away when leadership lacks autonomy.
They walk away when complexity relies on memory.
They walk away when the future relies on hope.

Most buyers won't say these words aloud.
But they will say them with silence.

The Structural Reason Buyers Walk Away

In the end, the reason buyers disappear is architectural:

The business cannot transfer without losing value.

Not losing revenue.
Not losing customers.
Not losing assets.
Losing *value*, the structural value of a company that can operate, grow, and thrive without the founder.

A company that depends on a founder is a job disguised as a business.
A company that functions without a founder is an asset.

Buyers buy assets.
They avoid jobs.

No buyer wants to inherit a job, especially one someone else is trying to escape.

The Deeper Lesson for Every Leader

The goal is not to impress buyers.
The goal is to become optional to your business.

Because when you become optional, three things happen:

Your valuation rises.
Your risk decreases.
Your freedom expands.

Sellability is not about selling.
It is about constructing a company that someone *would* buy, even if you never hand it over.

Because the architecture that attracts a buyer
is the same architecture that protects your legacy.

3XV in Due Diligence

Founders often imagine due diligence as a parade of accountants, lawyers, and analysts scrutinising spreadsheets and contracts. They believe valuation lives in EBITDA, margins, revenue forecasts, and financial discipline. And while these things matter, they are not what decides whether a buyer sleeps peacefully at night.

The real due diligence happens long before the accountants enter the building.
It happens in the rooms where buyers whisper to each other.
It happens in the questions they ask when you're not in the room.
It happens in the way they map your business against a framework you've never seen.

Every buyer conducts a 3XV assessment, silently.

Vision.
Value.
Vehicle.

Not the words, of course. They don't call it 3XV.
But they test the same three levers because these levers determine the one thing every buyer cares about:

Can this business continue creating value without the founder?

If the answer is yes, the deal accelerates.
If the answer is no, the deal dies, quietly.

VISION: The Buyer's First Test of Transferability

Vision is the first filter buyers use, because it tells them whether the company has direction beyond the founder's personality. They're not looking for inspirational phrases. They're looking for structural coherence.

A buyer once explained it to me this way:
"If the founder is the only person who can explain where the company is going, then the company has nowhere to go without him."

During due diligence, buyers look for evidence of Vision everywhere:

Do teams understand the company's long-term direction without rehearsed talking points?
Can senior leaders articulate strategy in the same language?
Does the roadmap look consistent with market reality?
Is the Vision resilient enough to survive leadership change?

Most founders fail this test without ever realising they were being examined.

I remember a buyer walking out of a meeting and saying, "They have ambition. But I didn't hear Vision."

The founder thought the meeting went brilliantly.

He didn't know the deal died in that one sentence.

VALUE: The Buyer's Test of Relevance and Differentiation

Buyers don't buy businesses.
They buy value engines, the mechanisms through which the company consistently creates customer value at a profit.

During due diligence, buyers search for answers to one question:

Is the Value proposition real, repeatable, and defensible without the founder?

They look for signals:

Do customers buy because of your product... or because of your charisma?
Does the company have a Value delivery system or does it rely on individual heroics?
Is the Value proposition clearly understood across teams without interpretation?
Is pricing consistent with the Value narrative or held together by the founder's confidence?
Does the business win because it is exceptional... or because the founder is exceptional?

When these answers are unclear, buyers disappear.

I once witnessed a buyer end an acquisition purely because the founder over-explained the company's Value proposition.
Not because he was wrong, but because no one else on his team could explain it.
To the buyer, this was the biggest red flag of all:
The Value wasn't distributed.
It lived inside one man.

Deals collapse quietly for this reason every day.

VEHICLE: The Buyer's Test of Scalability and Risk

If Vision is direction and Value is purpose, Vehicle is capability, the engine that determines whether the business can grow, replicate, and operate independently.

Buyers obsess over the Vehicle.
They won't admit it, but they do.

Because the Vehicle determines whether your business is an asset...
or a liability wrapped in revenue.

During due diligence, they examine:

Is your delivery model dependent on founder improvisation?
Is your operational engine robust enough to scale?
Are your processes documented or memorised?
Is decision-making distributed or trapped in a bottleneck?
Does the organisation break when pressure rises?
Is your success dependent on personality or architecture?

A buyer once told me, "We don't acquire companies. We acquire Vehicles. If the Vehicle can travel without the founder, we buy. If the Vehicle collapses without him, we walk."

Most founders believe numbers tell the story.
Buyers know Vehicles tell the truth.

The Meeting Where a Deal Died Before the Founder Entered the Room

I once sat with a private equity partner reviewing a company during due diligence. The founder was preparing to present. The room was quiet. Then the partner turned to me and asked:

"Moe, before we hear the pitch, does this business have a real Vehicle or is the founder the Vehicle?"

I paused.

He smiled. "Your silence tells me everything."

The deal did not proceed.

Not because of revenue.
Not because of systems.
Not because of profit.

179

But because the founder's identity was holding the architecture together.

Buyers will not inherit dependency.
They will not adopt risk.
They will not pay for a business that breaks when the founder leaves the room.

3XV reveals that instantly.

Why 3XV Becomes the Buyer's Quiet Risk Framework

Vision determines whether the company can navigate the next decade.
Value determines whether the company will remain competitive.
Vehicle determines whether the company can grow without collapsing.

When these three are aligned, buyers relax.
When they are misaligned, buyers vanish.

I've watched buyers ignore minor financial weaknesses because the 3XV structure was strong.

I've also watched buyers run from financially brilliant companies because the 3XV design was weak.

Buyers will forgive numbers.
They will not forgive architecture.

Because architecture is destiny.

The Structural Truth Most Founders Never Hear

Due diligence is not just financial.
Due diligence is architectural.

Buyers are not only asking:

"What is this company worth today?"
They are asking:
"What shape will this company be in after we remove the founder?"

If the business cannot answer that question confidently,
if the architecture collapses into silence,
the buyer walks.

Not loudly.
Not emotionally.
Not dramatically.

Just quietly.

And founders rarely understand why.

The Lesson for Leaders Who Want Real Optionality

If your company can survive the removal of your presence,
your intuition,
your decision-making,
your memory,
your relationships,
your charisma…

…then due diligence becomes easy.

Because 3XV becomes undeniable.

Vision gives confidence.
Value gives conviction.
Vehicle gives certainty.

And together, they give buyers what they need most:

**A business that works today
and will still work tomorrow
without the person who built it.**

That is the essence of sellability.
That is the heart of transferability.
That is the architecture buyers pay for.

Everything else is noise.

Founder Dependency, The Silent Killer of Value

If there is one structural weakness that destroys valuation faster than declining revenue, competitive pressure or market shifts, it is founder dependency. Every buyer fears it. Every private equity partner looks for it. Every advisor whispers about it. And every founder underestimates it, until the moment the deal collapses.

Founder dependency is not ego.
It is architecture.

It is the quiet, unintentional way a founder becomes the centre of gravity around which every decision, every relationship, every crisis, and every piece of institutional memory orbits.

Founders don't design this dependency.
They grow into it.

It begins innocently enough.
A founder knows the customer better than anyone else.
A founder can solve problems faster than anyone else.
A founder carries the culture, the vision, the standards, the intuition.
A founder feels responsible for everything the business has become.

And because the founder is good at these things, the organisation naturally leans on them.
Slowly.
Quietly.
Unnoticed.

Until the founder becomes the company's operating system.

That is when value begins to die.

The Illusion of Strength

Years ago, I worked with a founder whose company was admired across his industry. He was charismatic, deeply intelligent, and beloved by his customers. People would say things like, "He is the company." They meant it as a compliment.

It wasn't.

Behind the scenes, the business could not breathe without him.
He approved everything.
He negotiated every major deal.
He handled every crisis.
He anchored every relationship.
He made every strategic decision.

His leadership team admired him, but they were trapped.
No one could move without checking with him.
No one could decide without his blessing.
No one could lead without his shadow.

When he first considered selling, he was confident.
The financials were strong.
The market position was enviable.
The brand was respected.

But as the buyer conducted their internal assessment, I watched the energy shift.

They asked a few seemingly harmless questions:

"Who manages this relationship when the founder is away?"
"How are major decisions made?"
"Who holds the key client trust?"
"What happens if the founder takes time off?"

The founder answered all of them with pride:

"I do."
"I do."
"I do."
"I do."

He believed he was demonstrating commitment.
The buyer saw exposure.

When the buyer walked away, he was devastated.
"They loved everything," he said. "Why didn't they buy?"

"Because they weren't buying a business," I replied.
"They were buying you. And you're not for sale."

Why Founder Dependency Destroys Value

Buyers fear founder dependency because it creates three structural risks:

1. **Continuity Risk** – If the founder steps away, value collapses.

2. **Scalability Risk** – The company cannot grow because the founder is the bottleneck.

3. **Transfer Risk** – Knowledge lives in the founder's mind, not in the organisation.

No buyer wants to inherit a company where the founder's absence creates damage.

And here is the hardest truth for founders to accept:

Founder dependency feels like leadership…
but it behaves like fragility.

It makes the founder indispensable,
and the business unsellable.

The Day I Saw Dependency Collapse a Deal in 17 Minutes

I once witnessed a private equity partner terminate an acquisition in less time than it takes to drink a coffee.

The founder delivered a brilliant pitch, polished, inspiring, confident.
But when the partner began asking deeper operational questions, something became obvious.

No one else in the room could answer them.

The founder kept jumping in.
Not aggressively, instinctively.

After the meeting, the partner pulled me aside and said:

"Moe, we don't buy companies where the founder is still the engine."

I asked him how long it took to reach that conclusion.

"Seventeen minutes," he said.

Seventeen minutes.
After years of building the company, years of sacrifice, years of growth…
the deal evaporated because the architecture depended on one person.

Dependency destroys value long before anyone realises it.

Why Founders Don't See It Coming

Founder dependency is invisible because it hides behind competence.

The founder is fast.
The founder is knowledgeable.
The founder is trusted.
The founder is the problem-solver.

Everyone becomes accustomed to this rhythm.
It feels natural.
It feels efficient.
It feels like leadership.

But it isn't leadership.
It's load-bearing.

And load-bearing founders break long before the company does.

I once told a founder, "Your company doesn't have a leadership problem. It has a you problem, and it's killing your valuation."

He didn't like the sentence.
But he never forgot it.

The Shift That Changes Everything

The most valuable companies, the ones that attract buyers effortlessly, are not led by founders who carry everything.

They are led by founders who are structurally *optional*.

Not absent.
Optional.

A founder should shape direction, not carry operations.
A founder should create vision, not approve every decision.
A founder should build culture, not maintain it alone.
A founder should architect value, not deliver it personally.

When founders transition from being the centre of the business

to being the architect of the business,
value multiplies.

Buyers see independence.
Teams see empowerment.
Customers see stability.
The market sees strength.

And the founder gains something priceless:
freedom.

Freedom to choose.
Freedom to step back.
Freedom to sell, or not sell.
Freedom to lead without being consumed by the company they built.

The real killer of value is not competition.
Not market volatility.
Not pricing pressure.
Not even profit margin.

The real killer is dependency.

A company that requires its founder is not an asset.
It is a hostage situation with good branding.

But a company that can thrive without the founder?

That is a transferable, scalable, sustainable architecture,
and buyers pay a premium for that.

Because they're not buying a business.
They're buying certainty.

Because architecture isn't only structural, it's conative. Buyers know the
future of a business rests on the instinctive wiring of the people who will
carry it forward.

CHAPTER 9:
Diagnosing the Pillars Through the 3XV Lens

The Day I Found the Fracture No One Else Saw

There is a moment in every engagement where I know, without doubt, whether an organisation will scale or collapse. It rarely comes in a boardroom presentation, or in the numbers, or during a leadership offsite.
It comes in a pause.
A hesitation.
A gap in the architecture that everyone else has normalised.

One of the clearest examples happened with a £45M company in Manchester, a company admired in its industry, praised in awards ceremonies, and envied by competitors who assumed their rise was unstoppable. The leadership team believed they were preparing for the next phase of scale. They invited me in to "validate their strategy."

But from the moment I stepped into the boardroom, I felt a tension the numbers were hiding.

Beautiful dashboards.
Perfectly formatted slide decks.
Confident voices.
A leadership team that looked synchronised.

And yet… something felt off.

Not broken.
Not dysfunctional.
Just misaligned.
In a way that only becomes obvious when pressure increases.

They were presenting an ambitious three-year plan, doubling revenue,

expanding into Europe, diversifying products, enhancing customer experience. It all looked impressive. It all sounded coherent. But something inside me kept whispering:
The architecture cannot carry this.

I sat quietly, letting the room speak, letting their energy reveal the truth beneath the strategy. Most consultants jump in early, asking questions, sharing insights, proving relevance. But I've learned that the architecture speaks before the leaders do, if you know how to listen.

Halfway through the COO's presentation, the fracture announced itself.

It wasn't a mistake or a bad assumption. It wasn't a financial miscalculation. It wasn't even operational. It was a single sentence that passed unnoticed by everyone else in the room.

He said, almost casually,
"We just need the teams to adapt a little faster."

Adapt faster.
I felt the entire architecture tighten around those words.

Because *adaptation* becomes a problem only when **the Vehicle no longer fits the Vision**, and the organisation is compensating for structural misalignment.

I leaned forward slightly, not enough to interrupt, just enough to listen deeper.

As the COO continued, he described delays, inconsistencies, hesitation. He framed them as performance issues. He used phrases like "they need more accountability" and "we need to push harder."

But what he was describing was not a people problem.
It was a **Vehicle problem**.

The organisation wasn't resisting.
The organisation was signalling capacity limits.

The fracture came into full view moments later, when the CFO presented the customer churn analysis. The numbers weren't concerning, less than 4%. But his explanation was the tell.

He said, "Clients are leaving because we couldn't deliver what we promised as quickly as they expected."

Again, the room nodded. Again, they interpreted it as a performance gap.

But I saw something else:
a **Value fracture**, what the market believed they were buying was not what

the organisation was structurally able to deliver.

Value misalignment is a slow, quiet bleed.
By the time it becomes visible in metrics, the architecture below it has already shifted.

Then came the founder's presentation, the final piece of the diagnostic puzzle.

He spoke with passion about the company's future, new markets, new partnerships, new products, new expansions. He painted a picture of growth so vibrant that the room felt energised simply listening to him.

But halfway through, he slipped into a sentence that changed everything:

"To achieve this vision, we will need everyone to operate at a higher level."

There it was.
The fracture no one else saw.

**When Vision becomes aspirational instead of architectural,
the entire organisation begins to fracture under pressure.**

It wasn't that his Vision was wrong.
It was that his Vehicle and Value structure were not designed to support it.

They were scaling a dream, not a design.

I asked one simple question when he finished:

"Who else in this room can articulate your Vision in the same way you just did?"

Silence.

Not discomfort.
Not uncertainty.
Just... silence.

The COO looked at the CFO.
The CFO looked at the HR Director.
The HR Director looked at her notes.

No one spoke.

That silence was the fracture.

A Vision that cannot be shared cannot be executed.
A Value that cannot be delivered cannot be believed.

A Vehicle that cannot adapt cannot scale.

After a few seconds, I said gently,
"This is not a strategy problem. And it is not a performance problem.
It is a 3XV fracture, and it lives beneath everything you've presented today."

The founder frowned.
The COO sat back.
The CFO folded his arms in quiet realisation.

I continued:

"Your Vision has expanded.
Your Value has drifted.
Your Vehicle has stayed the same.
You are scaling at three different speeds."

The COO spoke first.
"What exactly are we missing?"

"You're missing alignment," I said. "Your Vision is outpacing your Vehicle.
Your Value proposition is evolving faster than your delivery capability. Your
operating model is designed for who you used to be, not who you are trying
to become."

The founder exhaled, a long, weary breath.

"This is why it feels like we're running uphill," he said.

"Yes," I replied. "Your teams aren't resisting change. They're protecting you
from collapse."

The room fell very still.
It always does at the moment the truth lands.

I walked them through the full 3XV diagnostic lens, something I had never
explained in that detail before:

Vision shows direction.
Value shows behaviour.
Vehicle shows capability.

"Right now," I said, "you have three truths pointing in three different
directions. That's why your people look tired. That's why your processes feel
heavy. That's why your decisions are slowing. You have a fracture that the
numbers hide beautifully, until the day they don't."

The founder looked at me and whispered,
"Why couldn't we see it?"

192

"Because you were inside the architecture," I said. "And architecture only reveals itself to those standing outside it."

The Reason This Chapter Exists

That day changed the company.
But it also changed my work.

It reaffirmed something I had learned long before but sometimes forget in the intensity of helping leaders chase scale:

The deepest fractures are architectural, not operational.
And 3XV is the only lens sharp enough to reveal them before they break.

This chapter exists because leaders believe diagnoses come from data.
They don't.
They come from alignment.
From coherence.
From structural truth.

The more complex a company becomes, the more invisible its fractures become,
until someone walks in with a lens designed to see what the organisation has stopped noticing.

That is 3XV.
That is architectural diagnosis.
That is the work we now begin together.

3XV as a Diagnostic Compass

When leaders talk about diagnosing problems, they usually think in terms of symptoms. Revenue softens, culture shifts, productivity dips, customers hesitate, decisions slow, meetings thicken, costs creep, and they assume each symptom requires a corresponding fix.

But after four decades of walking into boardrooms where everything looked fine but nothing felt right, I've learned the opposite:

Symptoms are misleading.
Patterns are revealing.
But 3XV is the compass.

3XV, Vision, Value, Vehicle, does not diagnose *what* is happening.
It diagnoses *why* it is happening.

It exposes the structural truth beneath the emotional stories leaders tell themselves.
It reveals the architecture beneath the explanations.
It turns a room full of opinions into a single coherent direction.

I didn't create 3XV to be clever.
I created it because organisations kept collapsing in ways that traditional tools simply couldn't predict.

And nothing crystallised this truth more than a moment years ago with a £90M company in Leeds.

The Boardroom Where Everyone Was Looking in the Wrong Direction

They had flown me in for what they called an "alignment session." The CEO said they were "slipping slightly," but nothing serious.
Whenever a leader says this, the alarms inside me ring softly.
Slippage is never slight. It is structural.

From the moment I walked into the room, I felt the tension.
Not toxic, tense.
Polite smiles stretched too wide.
Voices slightly too controlled.
A room where people were performing stability.

The CFO opened with a financial update.
A minor drop in margin.
A slight increase in churn.
Nothing dramatic.

But numbers never tell the story, they only confirm it.

Then the COO began speaking about operational challenges: recruitment delays, increased rework, handoff inconsistencies.
Again, nothing dramatic.
But inconsistency is the language of architectural drift.

As the conversation grew noisier, with each leader advocating for their preferred solution, more hiring, more process, more systems, more training, I sat back and listened.

Not to the noise.
To the pattern beneath it.

Because 3XV doesn't diagnose symptoms.
It reveals misalignment.

And misalignment always speaks through tension.

The CEO turned to me and said, "Moe, you've been silent. What do you think?"

I replied with a sentence that shifted the entire room:

"You're solving for the wrong layer."

Silence.
Then confusion.

"What layer should we solve for?" the CEO asked.

"Identity," I said. "And identity lives in Vision, Value, and Vehicle."

The room leaned in.

VISION: The Compass of Coherence

I began with Vision because Vision is always the first truth to fracture, quietly, invisibly, beneath the pressure of scale.

"Tell me," I said to the team, "what is your Vision now?"

Six people answered.
Six different interpretations.

Not contradictory, parallel.
And parallel is more dangerous than contradictory, because parallel looks aligned until the organisation starts moving.

I looked at the CEO. He looked down.

Vision is not a slogan.
Vision is a decision boundary.
Vision is the architecture of direction.

When Vision fractures, decisions fracture.
When decisions fracture, behaviour fractures.
When behaviour fractures, performance fractures.

And companies try to fix performance instead of direction.

3XV brings Vision back into focus, sharp, uncompromising, singular.

"Your Vision drifted," I said. "And when Vision drifts, everything else compensates."

The room fell eerily quiet.
Because they all knew it was true, even if they couldn't articulate it.

VALUE: The Compass of Behaviour

Next, I turned to Value.

"Why do customers choose you?" I asked.

The CMO answered with branding language.
The head of sales with product features.
The COO with delivery speed.
The CFO with pricing strategy.

Four answers.
All intelligent.
All wrong.

Because Value is not what you sell.
Value is the identity the customer recognises and returns for.

I pressed deeper:
"What is the one reason your best customers choose you over any alternative?"

They looked at each other.
Then at the table.
Then at me.

No one answered.

When a company cannot articulate why customers choose them, it is not a marketing problem.
It is a Value fracture.

When Value fractures, culture compensates.
Teams work harder.
Processes multiply.
People burn out.
Leaders escalate decisions.
Systems strain.

This is the unseen cost of Value drift.

Finally, the head of customer experience spoke quietly:
"Our customers choose us because of trust. Not speed. Not price. Trust."

The room shifted.
I felt it immediately, the click of truth landing.

"That's your Value," I said. "But your operations, messaging, and strategy are behaving as if your Value is speed. That misalignment is the real reason for your drift."

The CEO closed his eyes briefly.
That kind of moment is never comfortable, but it is always transformative.

VEHICLE: The Compass of Capability

Then came the part everyone avoids: **Vehicle**.

"What is your operating model designed to deliver?" I asked.

The COO replied confidently, "Consistency and efficiency."

But the symptoms told a different story.

If a Vehicle is designed for consistency:
Why were reworks increasing?
Why was churn rising?
Why were decisions escalating?
Why were managers overextended?

"Your Vehicle is designed for craftsmanship, not scale," I said.

The COO looked stunned.
The CFO leaned forward.
The CEO's face tightened.

"The problem," I continued, "is not your people. It is the shape of your engine."

A Vehicle that works beautifully at £30M collapses under the complexity of £90M.
A Vehicle that relies on memory cannot grow.
A Vehicle that depends on heroics cannot transfer.
A Vehicle that requires founder involvement cannot scale.

Every organisation outgrows its original Vehicle.
The mistake is assuming the Vehicle can stretch.
Vehicles do not stretch.
They crack.

"Your organisation is compensating for a Vehicle that no longer fits," I said.
"And your team is tired not because they are weak, but because they are carrying weight that the architecture should carry."

The CEO inhaled sharply.
Truth always lands first in the person carrying the company.

3XV Turns Complexity Into Clarity

The room that had been swirling with noise, blame, frustration, competing priorities, suddenly quieted.

Because 3XV had mapped the truth:

Vision had drifted.
Value had diluted.
Vehicle had not evolved.

Three fractures.
One truth:

They were no longer the company their architecture was built for.

This is why 3XV is a diagnostic compass.
Not because it simplifies complexity.
But because it reveals direction.

After years of consulting, I once believed diagnosis was about analysis.
It isn't.
It's about alignment.

3XV aligns every question you ask, every decision you make, every structural redesign you consider.

Instead of asking:

What's wrong?
Who is responsible?
Where is the problem?

3XV asks:

Is our Vision coherent?
Is our Value consistent?
Is our Vehicle capable?

Those three questions expose the architecture instantly, and truthfully.

The Moment the Compass Reoriented the Entire Company

The CEO finally spoke.

"Moe," he said softly, "how long has this fracture been here?"

"Eighteen months," I replied.

He nodded, almost relieved.
Because architectural fractures are not failures.
They are revelations.

Once you can see them, you can fix them.
Once you fix them, everything accelerates.
Once everything accelerates, scale becomes inevitable.

That company didn't need more meetings.
They didn't need more people.
They didn't need more process.
They didn't need more enthusiasm.

They needed a compass.
They needed 3XV.

Within twelve months, they rebuilt the Vehicle.
Realigned the Value proposition.
Sharpened the Vision.
And the friction that once felt unbearable evaporated.

Not because they worked harder,
but because the architecture finally pointed in one direction.

That is the power of 3XV.

It is not a tool.
It is not a model.
It is not a framework.

It is the compass that reveals truth in a landscape where leaders often drown in noise.

And once you learn to navigate with it,
you will never misdiagnose your organisation again.

The Pillar Baseline Assessment

There comes a point in every leadership journey where instinct is no longer enough.
For a while, sometimes years, instinct carries you.
It helps you make fast decisions.
It helps you build momentum.
It helps you survive the chaos of early growth.

But when a company crosses into real scale, the eight-figure weight class, instinct becomes blurry. Even dangerous. The very instincts that once propelled you forward begin to distort your perception. Success becomes noise. Patterns become harder to see. Signals disappear beneath activity. The pressure to make the right call increases, even as clarity decreases.

That is the moment when every founder, every CEO, every board member eventually asks the same question:

"Where exactly are we?"

Not metaphorically.
Structurally.

Because until you know where you stand today, you cannot design where you're going tomorrow.

This is why I created the Pillar Baseline Assessment, not as a theoretical exercise, but as the first moment of architectural truth-telling inside an organisation. The Five Strategic Pillars, Systemisation, Staffability, Scalability, Sustainability, and Sellability, are not abstract frameworks you read about in a book. They are the load-bearing structures of your business. If any one of them weakens, everything above it shakes.

The Baseline Assessment is the first time leaders see their company the way I see it when I walk into a boardroom.

And the first time they realise the Pillars do not operate independently.

They pull against each other.
They compensate for each other.
They hide each other's fractures.
They expose each other's weaknesses.

Which means you cannot fix what you cannot see, and you cannot see what you have not measured.

Why Most Leaders Misjudge Their Pillars

When I ask a founder to self-assess the strength of their Pillars, they almost always overestimate.

Not because they are arrogant, but because they are close.

Closeness blurs clarity.

A founder sees effort where I see inefficiency.
A founder sees loyalty where I see dependency.
A founder sees ambition where I see structural mismatch.
A founder sees activity where I see drift.

It's not their fault.
When you are inside the architecture, the walls feel bigger than they actually are.

One CEO once told me, "Our systems are strong. Our people are strong. Our scalability is strong."
Within twenty minutes of examining the architecture, it became clear that none of the three were structurally aligned.

He hadn't lied.
He had simply been living *inside* the problem for too long.

The Baseline Assessment pulls leaders *outside* the architecture, for the first time, so they can finally see what the company has been trying to tell them.

How the Baseline Assessment Actually Works

The assessment is not a score.
It is not a test.
It is not a diagnostic tool in the traditional consulting sense.

It is a structural mirror.

Each Pillar is examined through two questions:

1. What weight is this Pillar currently carrying?
2. What weight was this Pillar designed to carry?

Between those two questions lies the truth.

Because it is never the visible weight that breaks a company,
it is the invisible weight the Pillar was never built to bear.

Take Systemisation.
Many teams believe they have good systems because things get done.
But if "getting things done" requires heroics, improvisation, memory, or
escalation, the Systemisation Pillar is not load-bearing, it is decorative.

Or Staffability.
A company might have fantastic people, brilliant managers, strong loyalty.
But if the leadership structure cannot absorb new load, new decisions, or new
growth, the Staffability Pillar is weakened, even if morale looks high on the
surface.

Scalability is the one most founders confidently overrate.
They assume growth equals scalability.
It doesn't.

Growth is movement.
Scalability is architecture.

Movement is easy.
Architecture is not.

The Baseline Assessment forces the organisation to confront whether it is
moving fast because the structure is strong, or because the people are strong
enough to compensate for weak structure.

That difference is everything.

The Company That Thought They Were a "Strong 4"

A few years ago, a founder brought his senior team together for what he believed was a celebratory moment.
He said they would rate each Pillar on a scale of 1 to 5.
He expected high marks.

Most teams do.

They began with Systemisation.
The COO rated it a four.
The CFO gave it a five.
The HR Director, a three.
The founder, a five.

Then I asked the quietest person in the room, the operations lead, what score she would give.

She hesitated.
Looked at the table.
Then said quietly, "Two."

The room fell silent.

"Why two?" I asked gently.

She said, "Because the system only works when everyone is at 100%. The moment one person is off sick, the whole thing breaks. That's not a four. That's not a five. That's a two."

She was right.
The Pillar wasn't strong, the people were strong.
They were compensating.

The founder stared at her, stunned.
Not because she was wrong, but because he had never seen it.

This is what the Baseline Assessment does.
It gives voice to truths that never emerge in normal conversation.
It reveals the fractures the organisation has been stepping over.
It exposes the patterns leaders have normalised.

And it levels the room.

Everyone becomes equal in the presence of truth.

The Day a Board Realised How Outgrown Their Architecture Had Become

Another company, a £70M firm in Birmingham, entered the Baseline Assessment convinced their biggest weakness was Staffability.

They believed they needed better recruitment, stronger managers, clearer roles.

But the assessment revealed something entirely different.

Their Staffability Pillar was not weak, it was overloaded.
Their Systemisation Pillar was weak, and it was dumping its weight onto people.
Their Scalability Pillar was inconsistent, so people were improvising.
Their Sustainability Pillar was under strain, so leaders were firefighting.
Their Sellability Pillar had degraded quietly because the founder remained the escalation point.

Staffability wasn't the problem.
It was the symptom.

Their people were exhausted because they were carrying the weight of three misaligned Pillars.

One board member whispered, "We've been blaming the wrong thing for two years."

He was right.

The Baseline Assessment does not tell you what is *wrong*.
It tells you what is *true*.
And the truth is always more useful than the problem you think you have.

Why the Baseline Assessment Must Come Before Any Strategic Plan

I no longer begin any engagement with strategy.
Strategy built on misdiagnosis is architecture built on sand.

Before strategy comes truth.
Before truth comes clarity.
Before clarity comes the Baseline Assessment.

Once leaders see their Pillars honestly, without excuses, without performance, without ego, something shifts inside them.

They stop asking, "What should we do next?"

They start asking, "What must the architecture become?"

That transition is the beginning of real scale.

A founder once said to me, "Moe, this is the first time I've seen my company from above. Not from inside it."

And that is exactly what the Baseline Assessment is built to do:

To lift you above the architecture so you can see what the organisation has been carrying, what it can no longer carry, and what it must become to carry more.

Every company tells a story.
Every Pillar speaks that story in its own language.

Systemisation speaks through flow.
Staffability speaks through load.
Scalability speaks through capacity.
Sustainability speaks through resilience.
Sellability speaks through independence.

The Baseline Assessment translates these languages into one coherent truth.

Not a plan.
Not a strategy.
Not an opinion.

A map.

A map of where you stand now, and the architecture you must build next.

Because once you know your true baseline, scale stops being a dream.
It becomes inevitable.

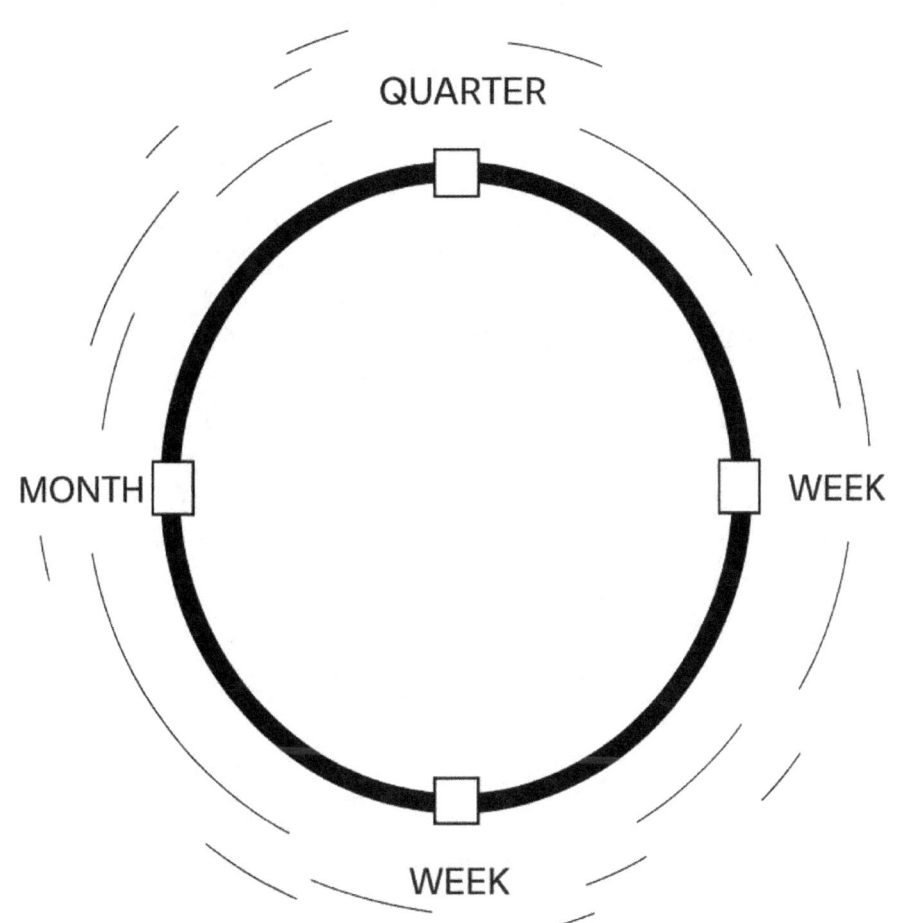

CHAPTER 10:
Designing Your Architecture Blueprint

Choosing the Right Pillar to Strengthen First

The moment a leader sees their Pillar Baseline Assessment with true clarity is the moment the real work begins.
And without fail, the very next question they ask is:

"Where do we start?"

They ask it with urgency.
Sometimes with excitement.
Often with anxiety.

Because once the truth is visible, the instinct is to fix everything at once, to accelerate, to repair, to rebuild, to catch up on years of drift.

But architecture is never rebuilt through urgency.
Architecture is rebuilt through sequence.

If there is one truth leaders struggle with more than any other, it is this:

You cannot strengthen all Pillars at the same time.
And you must never strengthen the wrong Pillar first.

Choosing the correct Pillar is not an operational decision.
It is an existential one.
It determines whether your organisation expands with clarity or collapses under confusion.

I've watched companies transform in months because they chose the right Pillar.
And I've watched companies lose years because they chose the wrong one.

The Mistake Almost Every Leader Makes

Most leaders instinctively choose the Pillar that is screaming the loudest.

If staff are burning out, they assume Staffability is the issue.
If revenue is flattening, they assume Scalability needs work.
If customers are drifting, they assume Value has weakened.
If culture is tense, they assume Sustainability is breaking.
If investors are circling, they assume Sellability needs to improve.

These seem like logical conclusions.
They are not.

They are emotional conclusions.

The loudest Pillar is rarely the weakest Pillar.
It is simply the one carrying the most visible weight.

The *weakest* Pillar is the one transferring its weight to all the others.

And that Pillar reveals itself not through noise, but through load.

I once worked with a company where the entire leadership team insisted their Staffability Pillar was broken. They were exhausted. People were leaving. Managers were overwhelmed. It felt obvious.

But when we looked deeper, we discovered the Staffability Pillar wasn't weak, it was overcompensating for a collapsed Systemisation Pillar.

They didn't need more people.
They needed less chaos.

Only when the flow architecture was rebuilt did the people stop collapsing under the strain.

If we had strengthened Staffability first, they would have hired more people into dysfunction.
More bodies.
More friction.
More cost.
More burnout.

The wrong starting point creates architectural noise.
The right starting point creates architectural acceleration.

The Question That Reveals Where to Begin

When a founder asks, "Which Pillar should we strengthen first?"
I never answer directly.

Instead, I ask:

"Which Pillar is currently carrying weight it was never designed to carry?"

That question cuts through noise like a blade.

It shifts the conversation away from symptoms and toward structure.
Away from emotion and toward engineering.
Away from leadership frustration and toward architectural truth.

And every time, the answer emerges with surprising speed.

Sometimes Systemisation is the one overloaded, a company drowning in decisions, improvisation, and memory-based processes.

Sometimes Staffability is carrying weight that belongs to broken flow, unclear roles, or founder dependency.

Sometimes Scalability is cracking because the Vision has grown while the Vehicle has not.

Sometimes Sustainability is straining because the company has been sprinting for too long, ignoring drift, fatigue, and structural erosion.

Sometimes Sellability is screaming because the business cannot step out of the founder's shadow, and everyone knows it except the founder.

The Pillar that carries the wrong weight is always the Pillar you begin with.

Because once you remove the weight it should never have been carrying, every other Pillar rises.

The Boardroom Where Choosing the Wrong Pillar Would Have Cost Them Three Years

A few years ago, I sat in a boardroom in Edinburgh with a company racing toward £60M.
The founder believed their Scalability Pillar needed strengthening.
Sales were growing.
Demand was increasing.
The pressure to expand was everywhere.

"If we don't scale now," he said, "we'll lose momentum."

Everyone nodded.

Everyone except me.

Momentum is dangerous when the architecture is unprepared.

So instead of discussing scale, I asked one quiet question:

"Why are your decisions slowing?"

The room froze.

They knew decisions were slowing.
They had normalised it.
Explained it.
Justified it.

But they had not questioned it.

The COO spoke slowly:
"We're relying too much on the founder for approvals."

"That's not a scalability issue," I said.
"That is a Staffability issue rooted in Systemisation."

The founder leaned back, silent.

They wanted to scale.
They were not ready to scale.

Had they strengthened Scalability first, they would have accelerated straight into a structural bottleneck.
Three years of delay.
Millions in cost.
Possibly a collapse.

Instead, they started at Systemisation,

then Staffability,
then Scalability.

Eighteen months later, they scaled effortlessly into Europe.

Sequence is everything.

Architecture Behaves Like a Spine

The Five Pillars are not independent columns.
They are a spine.

If one vertebra shifts, the entire body adjusts.
If one weakens, the others compensate.
If one carries too much, the structure bends.

I've seen companies where Systemisation was so broken that Staffability looked like the problem.

Companies where Staffability was so stretched that Scalability looked impossible.
Companies where Sustainability was so eroded that Sellability seemed unattainable.
Companies where Sellability was collapsing because Vision had drifted and no one could articulate the Value proposition anymore.

Symptoms rise where the load appears.
Truth sits where the load originates.

When you choose the wrong starting Pillar, you treat the symptom and ignore the origin.
When you choose the right one, the entire spine realigns.

How I Help Leaders Choose Their Starting Pillar

I take them through three reflective questions, quietly, slowly, without rushing the moment:

1. Which Pillar is absorbing weight from all the others?
This is the compensation Pillar, the one you do NOT fix first.

2. Which Pillar is transferring weight onto the others?
This is the origin Pillar, the one you MUST fix first.

3. Which Pillar, if strengthened today, would create the greatest flow tomorrow?
This is the leverage Pillar, the one that accelerates everything.

When leaders answer these honestly, the path becomes obvious.
Sometimes painfully obvious.

A founder once whispered after this exercise,
"I've been fixing everything except the one Pillar causing the damage."

That moment of truth is priceless.
It resets the entire trajectory of the business.

What Happens When You Choose Correctly

When the right Pillar is strengthened first:

Clarity returns.
Flow resumes.
Decisions accelerate.
People breathe again.
Meetings shorten.
Ownership rises.
Drift evaporates.
Confidence returns.

And the organisation begins to scale without forcing scale.

Because architecture, when aligned, creates its own momentum.

The founder sees it first.
The team feels it next.
The numbers confirm it later.
The market believes it eventually.

Strengthening the right Pillar first is not operational strategy.
It is structural liberation.

The Quiet Conclusion

Choosing the right Pillar is not the beginning of the redesign.
It is the beginning of the truth.

Once you choose correctly, the architecture begins to reveal its potential, not in explosive leaps, but in quiet alignment.

Because architecture doesn't announce itself with noise.
It announces itself with ease.

The right Pillar removes friction.
The wrong Pillar multiplies friction.

And the simplest way to determine where to begin is still the most powerful:

**Start where the unseen weight originates,
not where the visible weight appears.**

That is how architecture transforms.
That is how companies grow.
That is how leaders evolve.

One Pillar at a time.
In the right sequence.
By design, never by accident.

Trade-Offs, Pain Points, and Tough Calls

When leaders begin redesigning their organisational architecture, they expect clarity to feel liberating.
And eventually, it does.
But the part no one warns them about, the part consultants often gloss over because it makes the work uncomfortable, is that clarity always brings pain before it brings progress.

Architecture demands trade-offs.
Architecture exposes what must break so something better can be built.
Architecture forces decisions leaders avoided long before the assessment made them unavoidable.

I've walked more than a thousand leaders through this stage, and every one of them hits the same wall, the moment where they realise the price of designing a scalable company.

Because the real cost of growth is never money.
It is the pain of choosing.

The Day a Founder Realised What His Growth Would Really Cost Him

A founder in the Midlands once said to me, "Moe, I want to scale, but I want to keep everything the same."

I smiled gently.
"I understand," I said. "But you cannot grow without changing what growth exposes."

He frowned.
"What does that mean?"

"It means the architecture you built to survive your early years cannot carry the weight of your future."

He paused, then whispered, "So what do I have to give up?"

I looked him in the eye.
"Something you care about."

He didn't like the answer.
No leader ever does.

Because the truth is this:

Every strategic redesign begins with a loss.
Every scalable architecture requires a sacrifice.
Every evolution demands letting go.

Growth is not addition.
Growth is substitution.
The removal of what no longer serves the next level.

When the founder finally accepted this, he made three tough calls, each one painful, each one necessary, each one liberating.

He upgraded a loyal but misaligned leader.
He redesigned a beloved process that had become a bottleneck.
He shifted his role from operator to architect, losing the comfort of control.

Those three sacrifices unlocked three years of stalled progress.
But each one hurt before it healed.

216

Why Trade-Offs Are the Currency of Scale

Trade-offs are unavoidable because architecture is finite.
Every system, every person, every structure has limits.
When you strengthen one Pillar, others must adjust.
When you raise capacity in one area, you expose limits in another.

Most leaders try to avoid this reality.
They want win–win outcomes.
They want harmony.
They want everyone to stay comfortable.

But scale does not arrive through comfort.
It arrives through clarity.

And clarity demands decisions that cost you something:

A system that once felt good must be dismantled.
A leader who feels loyal must be repositioned.
A structure that kept you safe must be expanded.
A process you built with pride must be replaced.
A way of working that once defined you must be surrendered.

When I tell leaders this, they sometimes push back.

"Isn't there a way to grow without disruption?"

There isn't.

Even nature grows through disruption, old cells die to make room for new ones.

Organisations are no different.

The Pain Points That Reveal the Next Step

When redesigning an organisation, the pain points are not signals of failure.
They are indicators of where the architecture is misaligned, or too small.

The pain tells you what must change.

Pain Point #1: The People Who Carried You Cannot Carry the Next Chapter

This is the quiet heartbreak of leadership.

Founders often realise that someone who was perfect for the £3M or £10M stage simply cannot perform at £30M or £50M. Their loyalty is unquestionable. Their dedication is deep. But capacity is not a moral quality, it is a structural reality.

One founder once said to me, "I feel guilty even thinking about replacing him."

I replied, "You are not replacing him. You are replacing the version of the company he helped build."

He closed his eyes, because the truth hurt, but it also freed him.

Pain Point #2: Letting Go of Control

Every founder has a moment where letting go feels like losing identity.

When the company grows, decisions must decentralise.
Leadership must distribute.
Ownership must shift.

This transition always stings, because the founder must step back from the comfort of being needed and step into the discomfort of being optional.

And being optional is the only path to Sellability and true scale.

Pain Point #3: Killing Processes You Personally Built

I once watched a founder cling to a process he had designed fifteen years earlier, a brilliant system at the time, but now a constraint.

"It still works," he insisted.

"No," I said. "You still make it work."

The system wasn't functioning.
He was compensating.

When he finally let it go, the company's operational weight dropped by 27% in three months.

But he mourned it for weeks, because it felt like letting go of a piece of his identity.

Pain Point #4: Outgrowing Your Current Vehicle

This one is the most painful of all.

Sometimes the business model itself, the Vehicle, is the problem.
Not the team.
Not the product.

Not the process.

The Vehicle simply cannot scale to where Vision is pointing.

This realisation can be devastating.

I've seen founders cry when they realised their beloved model could carry them no further.
But I've also seen these same founders break records after embracing a new Vehicle.

Pain precedes power.
It always has.

The Tough Calls That Separate Leaders From Survivors

The difference between leaders who scale and leaders who stagnate is rarely intelligence.
It is willingness.

Willingness to face what is uncomfortable.
Willingness to choose what is costly.
Willingness to sacrifice what feels safe.
Willingness to redesign what was once sacred.

The toughest calls often include:

Removing a long-standing manager who no longer fits the architecture.
Shifting power away from the founder and into leadership teams.
Rebuilding the organisational chart for who you are becoming, not who you have been.
Redesigning compensation to reward behaviour, not tenure.
Parking initiatives that drain energy but feed ego.
Ending relationships with customers who damage the architecture.
Stopping growth to rebuild strength.

Each one of these choices hurts.
Each one is essential.

Because architecture that avoids pain becomes architecture that collapses.

The Truth Leaders Eventually Accept

After guiding thousands of leaders through this stage, I've come to believe there is a quiet sentence that defines leadership at scale:

"The cost of clarity is letting go of what no longer serves the future."

Once leaders accept this, everything changes.

Their decisions sharpen.
Their emotions steady.
Their teams breathe.
Their architecture strengthens.
Their Pillars realign.
Their company accelerates.

Not because the pain disappeared,
but because it finally had purpose.

Trade-offs become investments.
Pain becomes insight.
Tough calls become turning points.

And architecture begins to behave like architecture,
carrying weight, not creating it.

The Quiet Ending Truth

Designing the organisational blueprint is not an intellectual exercise.
It is an emotional discipline.

You will have to let go of things that once defined you.
You will have to make decisions others avoid.
You will have to step into discomfort so the company can step into scale.

And when you finally choose correctly,
when you make the tough calls not from fear, but from clarity,
your organisation will begin to rise in ways you once thought required force.

Architecture doesn't need force.
It needs truth.
Truth expressed through trade-offs.
Truth expressed through courage.
Truth expressed through decisions only you can make.

And this chapter exists for one purpose:

To prepare you for the moment when those decisions arrive
— because they always do.

The Three-Year Architecture Plan

Every founder dreams of momentum, the feeling that the organisation is not just moving forward, but moving with purpose. Yet the moment they begin redesigning their architecture, they often expect change to be immediate, as if structure responds to enthusiasm rather than sequencing.

It never does.

Architecture has its own rhythm.
It bends slowly.
It strengthens gradually.
It transforms in layers.
It reveals truth one decision at a time.

This is why every serious redesign I've guided over the past four decades rests on the same foundation: a three-year architecture plan. Not a Gantt chart. Not a set of milestones. Not a project plan dressed up as transformation. A genuine, structural evolution measured through capacity, cohesion, clarity, and behavioural change.

Three years is not an arbitrary timeframe.
It is the minimum period required for an organisation to shed its old identity, stabilise its new one, and scale without fracturing.
It is long enough for change to take root, but short enough to maintain urgency.
It gives leaders room to breathe while ensuring the architecture doesn't drift.

Whenever I present this to a client for the first time, they respond with the same mixture of surprise and relief.

"Three years?"
"Yes."
"Not one?"
"No."
"Not six months?"
"Absolutely not."
"Why so long?"
"Because your architecture has to unlearn before it can evolve."

And that is the truth no one tells leaders: before a company can scale, it must first unbuild the habits, assumptions, and structures that once made sense, but no longer do.

Year One: Stabilisation and Structural Truth

Year One is never glamorous.
It is the year leaders confront themselves.

I tell them, "Year One is the year where the organisation stops pretending."

In this year, the work is not about acceleration. It is about alignment. Leaders identify the Pillar that must be strengthened first. The company begins removing the weight that Pillar should never have carried. Teams learn new rhythms. Decisions decentralise. Systems stabilise. The fog lifts.

But Year One is also the year the ghosts appear.

Old habits resist change.
Legacy processes cling to power.
People who were comfortable in chaos struggle with clarity.
Managers who thrived on firefighting suddenly feel exposed.

The founder almost always has a moment, and it usually happens around month eight, where they say, "This is harder than I expected."

And I tell them, "That's how you know you're on the right path."

Because architecture reveals its resistance before it reveals its strength.

By the end of Year One, the organisation breathes differently. Not faster, cleaner. The noise reduces. The emotional volatility decreases. Meetings become shorter. Decisions stop ricocheting. The Pillar chosen as the foundation begins to settle.

It is not transformation.
It is readiness.

And readiness is a structural achievement.

Year Two: Expansion and Capacity Building

Year Two is the year everything begins to move.
Teams feel lighter because the system is carrying weight that people used to carry.
Managers step into authority they never had.
Processes behave without constant supervision.
The founder becomes optional in areas that once consumed them.

This is the year leaders start to say things like, "I feel like I can finally think again."
It is the year creativity returns, not as a spark but as a capacity.
The organisation stops reacting and begins designing.

If Year One is about stabilising the architecture,
Year Two is about strengthening it.

This is where the next Pillar often becomes the focus, usually Staffability or Scalability. Leaders evolve roles, reshape teams, redesign incentives, and expand decision-making capabilities. Behaviour changes before strategy does. And that is exactly how it should be.

Because architecture always shifts behaviour first, results second.

This is also the year where I watch founders undergo their own internal restructuring.
They stop being the lead operator.
They become the architect.

Some fight this transition.
Some embrace it.
All grow because of it.

Year Two is the year momentum returns, not emotional momentum, but structural momentum.
The kind that lasts.

Year Three: Acceleration and Strategic Confidence

Year Three is where organisations finally step into the future they once fantasised about but could never architecturally support.

The third year is the year leaders get brave.

They make decisions the old structure was too fragile to hold.
They pursue opportunities the old Vehicle could not carry.
They embrace markets, models, and strategies that once felt risky, because now the architecture can absorb the impact.

This is the year the company begins scaling by design rather than scaling by effort.

A founder once said to me during his third year, "I feel like someone removed a ceiling I forgot was there."

I replied, "No ceiling was removed. You finally built the walls strong enough to climb beyond it."

Year Three is not the end of transformation.
It is the beginning of stability at scale.

The company becomes:

Simpler to run.
Easier to lead.
Clearer to grow.
Stronger under pressure.
More valuable to buyers.
More attractive to talent.
More resilient to shocks.

By this stage, the architecture no longer resists growth, it creates it.

And the founder is no longer asking, "Where do we start?"
They're asking, "What can this company become now that we're not holding it back?"

That question is the truest sign of structural maturity.

Why Three Years — Not One, Not Five

One year is too short.
It favours cosmetic change over structural change.
It rewards motion over transformation.
It builds hope instead of architecture.

Five years is too long.
It dilutes urgency.
It creates drift.
It shifts leadership focus from transformation to maintenance.

Three years strikes the balance.

It respects the time architecture needs to evolve.
And it demands the discipline leaders need to stay the course.

Three years is the minimum investment required to redesign how an organisation behaves under pressure, how it carries weight, how it scales, and how it sustains itself.

Anything less is decoration.
Anything more is delay.

The Emotional Journey of the Three-Year Plan

I've watched this journey unfold hundreds of times.

Year One feels like truth.
Year Two feels like progress.
Year Three feels like freedom.

Freedom from firefighting.
Freedom from dependency.
Freedom from structural fragility.
Freedom from decisions that should never have reached the founder in the first place.

But above all:

Freedom to build the company you always imagined without sacrificing your life to run it.

The three-year architecture plan is not about time.
It is about identity.
It is about becoming the organisation your Vision requires,
your Value promises,
and your Vehicle can finally carry.

The companies that embrace this journey rise.
The companies that resist it repeat the same year forever.

CHAPTER 11:
Operating Rhythm, The Enforcement Layer

Why Architecture Drifts Without Rhythm

Architecture does not collapse overnight.
It drifts.
Quietly. Invisibly. Gradually.
Until one day, the weight becomes too much, and a leader wonders, "How did we get here?"

Most organisations do not fall because they made one catastrophic mistake. They fall because the rhythm that once held the architecture together slowly dissolves, and no one notices until the consequences arrive.

I have seen beautifully designed companies lose their way not because their strategy was fragile, but because their operating rhythm was absent.
I have seen businesses with extraordinary potential weaken not through bad decisions, but through inconsistency.
I have seen leaders become overwhelmed not because the architecture was wrong, but because the architecture was never enforced through cadence.

Architecture is design.
Rhythm is discipline.
Without rhythm, design decays.

And if there is one truth leaders underestimate more than any other, it's this:

Your organisation does not rise to the level of its goals.
It rises, or falls, to the rhythm that enforces them.

The Day I Watched a Strong Architecture Slowly Unravel

I once worked with a company that had built one of the cleanest architectures I'd ever seen.
Clear Vision.
Coherent Value.
A powerful Vehicle.
Solid Pillars.
Clarity in roles.
Strength in culture.

For the first eighteen months, they operated with discipline.
Meetings had structure.
Metrics had meaning.
Decisions had owners.
The rhythm of the organisation was consistent, calm, and predictable.

Then something subtle happened.

They grew.
Headcount increased.
The founder became busier.
Leaders took on more responsibilities.
Meetings became longer.
Reviews became less frequent.
Decisions became more ad hoc.

Nothing dramatic.
Nothing alarming.
Just small deviations, tiny tremors in the rhythm.

When I returned for a review nine months later, the architecture was still intact, but the organisation felt heavier.

"Nothing is wrong," the founder told me.
"But nothing feels as easy as before."

That sentence, *nothing feels as easy as before*, is the first sign of rhythm decay.

Ease is not luck.
Ease is enforced structure.
And once the rhythm slips, ease evaporates.

When I looked deeper, the signs were everywhere:

Quarterly reviews had become bi-annual.

Weekly syncs were happening every eleven days.
Responsibilities had blurred.
Decisions were delayed.
People were improvising.
Energy felt inconsistent.

The architecture hadn't changed.
The rhythm had.

And rhythm, not architecture, is what sustains scale.

I told the founder, "Your architecture didn't break. Your operating rhythm slowed by ten percent. But ten percent degeneration, if left unchecked, becomes a structural slide."

He looked at me and said quietly, "I didn't realise rhythm mattered this much."

It always matters.
It is the invisible force that either holds complexity together or lets it drift into chaos.

Drift Is Not a Failure, It Is the Default State of Every Organisation

Leaders often assume drift is a symptom of weakness.
It isn't.

Drift is natural.
Expected.
Predictable.

Every organisation drifts unless something actively prevents it.

Why?

Because humans drift.
Habits drift.
Priorities drift.
Focus drifts.
Communication drifts.
Standards drift.
Decisions drift.
Teams drift.

And architecture, like gravity, is always either being strengthened or eroded.

The operating rhythm is what keeps drift from becoming destiny.

A leader once asked me, "Why do we need rhythm if the architecture is strong?"

I answered, "Because architecture is potential. Rhythm is practice. Potential has no power without practice."

Without rhythm:

The system relaxes.
The lines blur.
The clarity softens.
The standards loosen.
The metrics drift.
The responsibilities mutate.
The organisation begins improvising again.

And the entire structure, no matter how beautifully designed, begins returning to its pre-architectural state.

The operating rhythm is the enforcement layer, the behavioural spine, the metronome that keeps the organisation's heart beating at the tempo required for scale.

The Quiet Enemy of Leaders: Success Without Rhythm

One of the most dangerous phases in any company's life is the early stage of success.
Because success gives leaders the illusion that rhythm is optional.

When the numbers look good, rhythm feels rigid.
When growth is accelerating, cadence feels bureaucratic.
When teams are winning, meetings feel unnecessary.
When momentum is high, discipline feels like drag.

But momentum is deceptive.
Momentum makes leaders believe the organisation is stable when in reality it is simply being carried by enthusiasm, not architecture.

I once warned a CEO in London, "Your success is eroding your rhythm."
He smiled, thinking I was being overly cautious.

Nine months later, the cracks appeared.

"Why didn't anyone tell me this earlier?" he asked.

"I did," I said. "You were distracted by success."

Success hides drift.

Rhythm reveals it.

And the organisations that remain successful for decades are not the ones that innovate the most,
they are the ones that enforce rhythm relentlessly.

Why Leaders Resist Rhythm (Even When They Need It Most)

Most leaders, especially founders, resist rhythm for three reasons:

1. Rhythm Feels Like Loss of Freedom

Entrepreneurs thrive in flexibility.
Structure can feel suffocating.
They equate rhythm with constraint rather than clarity.

What they don't realise is that rhythm doesn't remove freedom,
it protects it.

The calmer the system,
the freer the leader.

2. Rhythm Feels Slow

Leaders want to move fast.
They assume cadence slows innovation.

But rhythm doesn't slow the organisation,
it synchronises it.

And synchronisation is the multiplier of speed.

3. Rhythm Requires Accountability

And accountability is uncomfortable.
Rhythm exposes what leaders don't want to see:

Missed standards.
Unmade decisions.
Unclear roles.
Emotional bottlenecks.
Architectural weaknesses.

Rhythm forces truth to surface,
and truth is rarely gentle.

But truth is always useful.

The Meeting That Proved Rhythm Is More Powerful Than Strategy

Several years ago, I facilitated a leadership meeting with a £120M company preparing for international expansion. Their strategy was flawless. Their architecture was solid. Their people were capable. Their market was ready.

But their rhythm was weak.

Meetings floated.
Priorities shifted weekly.
Reviews were infrequent.
Deadlines moved.
Owners rotated.

I told them, "Your strategy does not matter until your rhythm stabilises."

They resisted me.
They insisted their strategy would carry them.
They believed the clarity of the plan was enough.

Six months later, they returned, bruised, humbled, and wiser.

Their expansion had stalled.
Their delivery timelines slipped.
Their teams were confused.
The founder was exhausted.

"What did we miss?" the COO asked.

I said, "You tried to scale strategy without scaling rhythm."

Strategy gives direction.
Rhythm gives momentum.
Architecture gives capacity.

Remove rhythm, and the entire machine slows just enough to sabotage itself.

The Moment a Company Realises Rhythm Is Its First Safety Net

One of my private clients, a global logistics group, once told me something that has stayed with me:

"Moe, rhythm became the first time we felt safe."

Safe.
Not stable.
Not successful.
Safe.

Because rhythm does something subtle and powerful:

It makes the future predictable.
It makes pressure bearable.
It makes decisions timely.
It makes priorities clear.
It makes drift visible.
It makes leaders accountable.

Rhythm creates emotional safety inside operational intensity.

Without it, companies burn out.
With it, they accelerate without losing control.

Why Architecture Drifts Without Rhythm

Let me say it plainly:

Architecture is a blueprint.
Rhythm is the enforcement.
Without enforcement, architecture is theory.

Every time a leader delays a review, drift begins.
Every time a team skips a sync, drift accelerates.
Every time a decision is postponed, drift compounds.
Every time responsibility blurs, drift becomes cultural.

Drift is the enemy of scale because drift compounds downward.

And the only force powerful enough to counteract drift
is rhythm.

Rhythm is the habit of structure.
Rhythm is the guardian of clarity.
Rhythm is the metronome of performance.

Rhythm is the enforcement of architecture.

Rhythm is what ensures:

Vision remains direction.
Value remains consistent.
Vehicle remains capable.
Systemisation remains flow.
Staffability remains capacity.
Scalability remains structural.
Sustainability remains stable.
Sellability remains protected.

Rhythm is not the work.
Rhythm is what makes all the work count.

The Quiet Ending Truth

When I look back at the companies that scaled beyond anyone's expectations, they all shared the same trait:

They did not worship strategy.
They did not obsess over innovation.
They did not chase trends.
They did not rely on heroics.

They enforced rhythm.

And rhythm became the invisible architecture beneath the architecture, the force that kept everything aligned, cohesive, and moving.

So when leaders ask me,
"Moe, what stops architecture from drifting?"

The answer is simple:

Discipline.
Cadence.
Rhythm.

Because without rhythm, even the best architecture will eventually forget what it was designed to become.

The Week, Month, Quarter Cadence

Once leaders accept that rhythm is the enforcement layer of architecture, the next question naturally emerges:

"What rhythm should we actually run the company on?"

They expect a formula.
They expect a method.
They expect a checklist.

But architecture is not a checklist.

It is a breathing system that needs its own tempo, not too fast, not too loose. The perfect cadence is not the one that pushes the organisation the hardest. It is the one that keeps the architecture aligned without exhausting the people living inside it.

After forty years of walking into boardrooms where drift had already begun, I learned that a company's rhythm must be built around three cycles:

The Week.
The Month.
The Quarter.

These three intervals create the operational heartbeat of a company. Miss one beat, and nothing seems wrong. Miss two, and the organisation feels heavy. Miss three, and drift begins to set in. Miss more than three, and the architecture that once felt solid begins to soften.

A company's success is not measured in annual goals.
It is measured in weekly commitments, monthly recalibrations, and quarterly architectural alignment.

This tri-layer cadence is what keeps truth close.
It is what prevents drift.
It is what makes scale sustainable.

The Weekly Cadence — The Pulse of Execution

A business does not run on strategy.
It runs on weeks.

Everything a company becomes, good or bad, happens one week at a time. And yet most leaders allow weeks to unfold without structure, without priorities, without clear accountability.

A leader once told me, "Moe, our weeks feel like sprints with no finish

lines."
Exactly.
That is the consequence of rhythm absent at the weekly layer.

The purpose of the weekly cadence is simple:

To keep the organisation moving in alignment with the architecture.

Not faster.
Not harder.
Just aligned.

What a weekly cadence really does

A weekly cadence forces clarity.
Forces focus.
Forces decisions.
Forces accountability.

But it does something deeper:
It prevents small drifts from becoming large fractures.

Every week is an opportunity to correct course before the architecture bends under the weight of neglect.

The Weekly Leadership Sync

This is the anchor.

Not a long meeting.
Not a reporting session.
Not death by update.

A short, precise alignment ritual where leaders answer three architectural questions:

1. What must move this week?
2. What friction or drift emerged?
3. What decision or support is needed to keep flow moving?

That's it.

No theatrics.
No performance.
No unnecessary detail.

The weekly sync is the structural equivalent of checking the building's foundation every seven days.

The cracks reveal themselves early.
And early cracks are easy to fix.

A founder once told me, "This meeting feels too simple."
I replied, "That's why it works. Complexity destroys rhythm. Rhythm thrives in simplicity."

Weekly cadence is the pulse.
It keeps the organisation alive.

The Monthly Cadence — The Breath of Leadership

If weekly rhythm is tactical, monthly rhythm is structural.
This is where leaders step above the noise and observe the architecture from a higher vantage point.

Monthly cadence answers questions the weekly rhythm cannot:

Is the organisation behaving the way the architecture intended?
Is the load distribution across the Pillars healthy?
Are we drifting emotionally, operationally, or strategically?
Is the founder being pulled back into areas they should no longer touch?

Where the weekly cadence is about movement,
the monthly cadence is about maintenance.

The two are not the same.
Movement without maintenance creates chaos.
Maintenance without movement creates stagnation.**The Monthly Alignment Review**

This is where the leadership team examines each Pillar with quiet honesty.

Not deep dives.
Not lengthy reports.
Not finger-pointing.

A simple, structured conversation:

Systemisation: Is flow holding?
Staffability: Are people carrying weight the system should carry?
Scalability: Are decisions accelerating or slowing?
Sustainability: What fatigue or cultural drift is emerging?
Sellability: Is dependency increasing or decreasing?

This monthly look at the architecture is the difference between a company that evolves intentionally
and one that wakes up surprised by its own problems.

I once told a CEO, "If you skip a weekly meeting, drift begins.
If you skip a monthly meeting, drift compounds."

Monthly cadence is the breath.
It keeps the organisation conscious.

The Quarterly Cadence — The Reset of Architecture

Quarterly cadence is where leadership becomes architectural.
It is where the organisation stops running and starts evaluating.

Every ninety days, the company must pause, not to rest, but to reflect.

Because ninety days is enough time for patterns to emerge,
enough time for subtle fractures to widen,
enough time for the organisation to reveal whether the architecture is working
or silently straining.

Quarterly rhythm is not operational.
It is existential.

It answers questions like:

Is our Vision still the true north?
Has our Value drifted in the market?
Is our Vehicle still capable of carrying our promises?
Are the Pillars aligned or compensating for each other?
Where must we reinforce our architecture before the next quarter begins?

When leaders take quarterly cadence seriously, the company becomes unshakeable.
When they ignore it, problems accumulate silently until they explode loudly.

The Quarterly Architectural Review

This is not a performance review.
It is not a financial review.
It is not a planning workshop.

It is a truth session.

A quiet, honest, unfiltered conversation about the architecture of the company.

I insist on two rules:

238

1. **No sugar-coating.**
2. **No self-congratulation.**

Because architecture only improves when leaders speak truth without performance.

In one particular quarterly review, a founder in London turned to his CFO and said, "I think we've been lying to ourselves about how scalable our Vehicle actually is."

It wasn't said with blame.
It wasn't said with regret.
It was said with clarity.

Clarity that changed their entire trajectory.

Quarterly cadence is the reset.
It keeps the architecture honest.

How the Three Cadences Work Together

Weekly cadence keeps execution on track.
Monthly cadence keeps architecture aligned.
Quarterly cadence keeps the organisation evolving.

Most companies run only one of these rhythms well,
usually the weekly one.

And because they only run one, they feel constantly behind.

They sprint through weeks, drown in months, and collapse in quarters.

But when all three rhythms work together, something powerful happens:

Problems become predictable.
Decisions become faster.
People become calmer.
Leaders become clearer.
Strategy becomes simpler.
Architecture becomes resilient.

The organisation begins to live inside a frame that protects it from chaos.

A founder once said to me, "This cadence makes us feel ten years more mature."
I replied, "That's because cadence accelerates maturity faster than strategy."

Why Leaders Fail Without Cadence

The absence of rhythm creates four predictable consequences:

1. Drift Becomes Cultural

Small inconsistencies become norms.
What was once unacceptable becomes tolerated.
What was tolerated becomes normal.
What becomes normal becomes identity.

2. Architecture Weakens Quietly

Not through big mistakes.
Through tiny deviations repeated weekly.

3. Leadership Overextends

Because no cadence means no clarity.
No clarity means leaders compensate.
Compensation creates burnout.

4. Strategy Loses Power

Because strategy without rhythm is like a blueprint without builders.

I once told a founder,
"You don't need more strategy. You need more rhythm."

He looked at me for a long moment before whispering,
"That feels painfully true."

The Emotional Truth of Cadence

Leaders often misunderstand cadence as management.
It is not.

Cadence is leadership.
Cadence is care.
Cadence is protection.
Cadence is discipline.
Cadence is stewardship.

Cadence is the way a leader says to their organisation,
"We will not drift.
We will not lose ourselves.
We will not build this architecture only to let it collapse through neglect."

Weekly is commitment.

Monthly is calibration.
Quarterly is transformation.

When all three are honoured, organisations become unrecognisable,
not because of dramatic reinvention,
but because of consistent alignment.

The Quiet Ending Truth

The companies that scale sustainably and effortlessly are not the ones with
the most brilliant strategies,
the most charismatic leaders,
or even the most innovative ideas.

They are the ones that enforce rhythm without apology.

Because rhythm is the container that protects culture, the metronome that
protects flow, and the spine that protects architecture.

When leaders ask me,
"How do we ensure we never drift again?"

I give them the same answer, every time:

**"Honour the week.
Respect the month.
Rebuild every quarter."**

Do that, and architecture becomes destiny.

CHAPTER 12:
Compression, Turning Five-Year Goals Into Three

The First Time I Compressed a CEO's Timeline

There are moments in your career you never forget, not because of the result, but because of what the moment taught you about the limits you once believed were unbreakable.

For me, compression began not as a method, not as a strategy, not even as a possibility.

It began as an accident.

I didn't set out to compress a CEO's timeline.

I simply walked into a boardroom where the future was moving slower than the architecture could carry, and I asked a question that would redefine the next forty years of my work.

It was the late 1990s in London.

The company was already impressive: £40M turnover, strong margins, a respected brand.

They hired me to help shape their "five-year plan."

It made sense. Back then, five-year cycles were the norm. Markets moved slowly, competitors watched politely, technology behaved predictably.

Five years felt reasonable.

Five years felt strategic.

Five years felt safe.

But from the moment I sat down with the CEO, a brilliant, driven, battle-scarred leader named Richard, I could feel the tension between the timeline he was aiming for and the architecture he actually had.

He was tired.

Not visibly.

Not dramatically.
But the kind of tired only leaders who carry weight alone ever understand.

He said, "Moe, I want to grow this company from £40M to £80M in five years."
He said it with confidence, with logic, with the calm tone of a man who had rehearsed the sentence enough times that it felt true.

I nodded.
But something in me resisted.

Not the goal.
Not the ambition.
The timeline.

Five years…
The architecture did not need five years.

"What makes it a five-year target?" I asked him.

He frowned. I remember the exact way his fingers stilled on the table.

"What do you mean?" he replied.

"I mean… why five?"
He looked confused, almost defensive, but not in a hostile way.
In the way someone does when you tug a thread they didn't know was loose.

"That's how long it takes to double," he said.

"That's how long it *used* to take," I replied softly.

He leaned back, eyes narrowing, mind unfolding.

For the first time in my career, I spoke the sentence that would eventually define my entire methodology:

"What if the architecture you already have could carry you there in three?"

He laughed.
Not mockingly, almost kindly.
Like someone amused by a magician before seeing the trick.

But then he looked at me again and realised I wasn't joking.

"Three years?" he asked.

"Yes."

"How?"

I paused, because the truth was, I didn't yet have a system or a fully articulated blueprint.
But I had something I trusted more:
the instinct of a man who had spent decades watching structure behave differently from belief.

"Because your architecture is capable of more than your assumptions are allowing," I told him. "You're planning for the pace you've survived, not the pace your structure can carry."

He didn't respond.
He just stared at me with the expression leaders wear when something inside them shifts, quietly, powerfully, irrevocably.

The Walkthrough That Changed Everything

We walked through the business together.
Not with presentations.
Not with spreadsheets.
Just a slow, methodical exploration of weight, flow, and load.

I showed him how Systemisation was underutilised.
How Staffability was stronger than he realised.
How Scalability was being constrained by old mental models.
How Sustainability was silently improving through culture he had never credited himself for building.

And how Sellability, though he wasn't planning to sell, was already at a maturity level that most firms spent years trying to achieve.

He kept shaking his head as if seeing his company for the first time.

"It doesn't feel this strong," he said.

"That's because you've been carrying weight the architecture should have carried," I replied. "Once we shift that weight off your shoulders, you'll see the truth."

He looked at me, suddenly serious.

"So this is possible?"
"It's not only possible," I said. "It's inevitable, if we remove everything slowing the architecture down."

"But compressing five years into three…" he whispered, almost to himself. "Is that safe?"

And this is the sentence I told him, a sentence I still tell founders today:

"It's safer than sitting still for five years while your competitors learn to move faster."

He exhaled slowly, the long breath of a man letting go of a belief he had carried for too long.

Compression Begins the Moment Assumptions Break

We redefined the target.

Not £80M in five years.
£80M in three.

The board thought it was madness.
His CFO thought I was reckless.
His COO thought it was inspirational, but unrealistic.

Richard thought it was terrifying.

But he also thought it was true.

The moment a leader sees the architecture beneath their assumptions, their timeline collapses.

Not because we push harder.
But because architecture, when aligned, accelerates naturally.

That is the essence of compression.

The First Breakthrough Came Sooner Than Expected

Four months later, Richard called me, breathless.

"You're not going to believe this," he said.
"We've just unlocked a new contract worth fifteen percent of our annual revenue."

I smiled.
"I believe it."

"But we didn't even chase it," he said.

"You didn't need to," I replied. "Your architecture did."

This is the part leaders don't understand at first:

Compression doesn't come from doing more.
It comes from removing what slows you down.

When the friction disappears,
the organisation leaps.

Richard was stunned.

"This would never have happened under the five-year plan," he said.
"No," I told him. "Because the five-year plan was built on fear. The three-year plan was built on architecture."

The Hardest Moment in the Journey

Not every part of compression is uplifting.

There was a moment, around month ten, where the weight of the new timeline hit him hard.
We had removed layers of friction.
We had strengthened the Vehicle.
We had clarified Value.
We had aligned Vision.

But now the organisation was moving so quickly that Richard became the bottleneck.

He called me one evening, frustrated.

"Moe, I'm slowing them down," he said quietly.
"Yes," I replied. "And that's the best news we've had."

He didn't understand.

So I explained:

"When the architecture is faster than the founder, the company is finally ready to scale."

Silence.
Then laughter, tired, honest, cathartic.

"What do I do?" he asked.

"Step aside," I said. "Stop being the engine. Become the architect."

It was the hardest shift he ever made.
But it was the moment compression became real.

Three Years Later

They didn't hit £80M.
They surpassed it.

£94.7M.
In thirty-six months.
With lower stress, lower drift, less chaos, and a healthier organisation than they'd ever had.

Richard looked at me during our final review and said, "I spent two decades thinking growth was about pushing harder. It was never about pushing. It was about design."

He paused, then added:

"And it was never a five-year journey. It was always three. I just couldn't see it."

I smiled.

"That's what compression really is," I said.
"It's seeing what was possible all along."

What That First Experience Taught Me

From that moment, I stopped believing in traditional timelines.
I stopped accepting five-year thinking.
I stopped tolerating slow cycles.
I stopped assuming leaders needed time.
What they needed was architecture.

Compression isn't magic.
It isn't speed.
It isn't urgency.

Compression is structural integrity accelerating the organisation once friction is removed.

The day I compressed my first CEO's timeline was the day I realised:

Most leaders are not limited by capability.
They are limited by assumption.
By inherited timelines.
By outdated thinking.
By structures built for survival, not acceleration.

But once the architecture aligns,
once the load is redistributed,
once the Vehicle strengthens,
once the Pillars rise together…

time collapses.

And what leaders thought required five years
requires three,
sometimes even less.

Why 3XV Plus the Pillars Make Compression Possible

When people first hear the idea of turning five-year goals into three, they assume compression is a trick, a mindset shift, a productivity hack, or a burst of adrenaline disguised as strategy.

It's none of those things.

Compression is not speed.
Compression is alignment.
Compression is architecture finally behaving the way it was always capable of behaving.

When 3XV, **Vision, Value, Vehicle**, aligns with the Five Strategic Pillars, **Systemisation, Staffability, Scalability, Sustainability, Sellability**, something extraordinary happens:

Time stops being linear.

Instead of progress moving inch by inch through resistance, it begins to move in leaps because the structural drag disappears.

A company does not accelerate because people push harder.
A company accelerates because friction is removed from its architecture.

And that is what 3XV plus the Pillars create:
a frictionless organisational spine capable of carrying more weight, making faster decisions, and absorbing growth at speeds previously impossible.

But to understand *why* compression works, you must understand the forces that normally slow companies down, forces leaders often mistake for "reality" when they are simply symptoms of misalignment.

Most Companies Don't Fail to Grow — They Fail to Align

In four decades, I've never seen a company stuck because of lack of ambition.
I've seen companies stuck because of lack of alignment.

A leader will say, "We need five years to reach that target," without realising that the timeline is not dictated by the market,
it is dictated by the friction inside their own architecture.

Friction in Vision, where teams interpret direction differently.
Friction in Value, where the message to the market does not match what is delivered.
Friction in Vehicle, where the operating model cannot carry expansion.

And then the Pillars each begin compensating:

Systemisation compensates through more meetings.
Staffability compensates through more people.
Scalability compensates through heroic effort.
Sustainability compensates by absorbing emotional strain.
Sellability compensates by relying on founder memory instead of structural independence.

When these compensations accumulate, time stretches.
Growth slows.
Decisions thicken.
Progress feels heavy.
Targets extend.
Five-year plans become seven-year plans.
Seven-year plans become "whenever we get to it."

Companies do not fall behind because they lack capability.
They fall behind because capability is trapped behind architectural drag.

Remove the drag
and time compresses.

The Role of Vision in Compression: Direction Without Ambiguity

Vision accelerates an organisation not by inspiring people,
but by eliminating hesitation.

Hesitation is the invisible thief of time.

When Vision is unclear, leaders debate direction.
Teams overthink decisions.
Priorities shift weekly.
Projects expand without boundaries.
Everyone waits for someone else to clarify what matters.

Unclear Vision adds months, sometimes years, to a company's timeline.

But when Vision is structurally clean:

Everyone moves in one direction.
Small decisions become automatic.
Large decisions become simpler.
Teams stop second-guessing.
Execution becomes coherent.

Clarity removes delay.
Delay is the enemy of speed.

This is why compression begins with Vision, not a motivational "why," but
an architectural "where."

Because without directional certainty, acceleration becomes impossible.

The Role of Value in Compression: Focused Relevance

Compression is impossible when Value is diluted.

Most companies try to serve too many customer types, solve too many problems, or deliver too many promises.
This creates operational sprawl, brand confusion, and internal complexity.

Complexity slows everything.

But when Value sharpens, truly sharpens, something profound happens:

The organisation stops negotiating its identity.
The market stops hesitating.
The team stops improvising.
The product stops mutating.
The strategy stops expanding sideways.

Value coherence removes waste.
Waste consumes time.

A company with sharp Value moves like a blade.
A company with diluted Value moves like a sponge.

Compression demands blade behaviour.

The Role of Vehicle in Compression: A Structure Built for Acceleration

There is one truth I wish every leader understood:

**No matter how ambitious your Vision is,
your company will only grow at the speed of its Vehicle.**

If the Vehicle, your business model, delivery engine, and operational design, is built for linear growth, it will resist exponential goals.

If the Vehicle is built for stability, it will resist acceleration.
If it is built around people instead of processes, it will collapse under weight.
If it relies on the founder, it will stall long before scale.

But when the Vehicle is redesigned to support the Vision and deliver the Value:

Flow accelerates.
Capacity expands.
Costs decrease.
Decisions distribute.

Outcomes become predictable.
Speed becomes structural.

This is the point where leaders begin to experience the first real signs of compression:

"What used to take six months just took six weeks."
"We solved a problem in hours that used to take us weeks."
"Opportunities are coming faster than we can process them."

It feels like magic.
But it's not magic.
It's architecture doing what architecture does when freed from constraint.

How the Pillars Turn Alignment Into Acceleration

Once 3XV is aligned, the Pillars amplify the acceleration.

And this is where compression moves from theory to inevitability.

Systemisation Removes Operational Drag

Every organisation has invisible friction:

Rework
Handoffs
Email loops
Decision bottlenecks
Role confusion
Process ambiguity

Individually, these problems seem trivial.
Collectively, they slow the entire company by 20–40%.

Systemisation eliminates this drag by transforming chaos into flow.

Flow accelerates everything,
hiring, execution, customer delivery, decision-making.

This is why companies with strong Systemisation
hit goals months earlier
even without working harder.

They remove the drag everyone else accepts as normal.

Staffability Expands Leadership Capacity

Compression requires distributed ownership.

If decisions must rise to the founder, time expands.
If managers lack confidence, time expands.
If the team is unclear, time expands.
If the organisation needs reassurance, time expands.

But when Staffability is strong:

Leaders decide without escalating.
Teams solve without waiting.
Conflicts resolve without drama.
Performance rises without pressure.

Companies accelerate when the founder is no longer the bottleneck.

Compression becomes possible when leadership becomes collective rather than concentrated.

Scalability Turns Growth Into Multiplication

When Scalability is weak, every new opportunity adds strain.
More revenue means more stress.
More customers means more complexity.
More projects means more risk.

But when Scalability is strong:

Every new customer strengthens the system.
Every revenue increase improves efficiency.
Every expansion clarifies the architecture.

This is where compression becomes unavoidable,
because scale begins to create its own momentum.

The company stops adding
and starts compounding.

Sustainability Creates Stability During Acceleration

Acceleration without resilience destroys companies.

Some organisations move fast, briefly,
then collapse from exhaustion, burnout, or cultural erosion.

Compression requires emotional stamina.

Sustainability ensures:

People stay strong.
Culture holds its shape.
Stress doesn't become identity.
Leaders don't hide struggles.
Teams don't quietly break.

This Pillar ensures speed does not cause damage.
It protects the architecture during acceleration.

Without Sustainability, acceleration becomes self-destructive.
With Sustainability, acceleration becomes normal.

Sellability Makes the Architecture Transferable

Compression is not just about speed.
It's about building a company that can grow without the founder holding it together.

Sellability ensures:

The founder becomes optional.
The company becomes independent.
Leadership is distributed.
Knowledge is embedded in systems.
Decisions are structural, not personal.

A company becomes compressible
the moment it becomes transferable.

Because transferability is maturity,
and maturity compresses time.

The Real Reason 3XV + the Pillars Create Compression

Most business methodologies add complexity.

3XV plus the Pillars remove it.

They remove friction.
They remove delay.
They remove dependency.
They remove inconsistency.
They remove confusion.
They remove emotional decision-making.
They remove architectural drag.

And when drag disappears, acceleration becomes natural,
not forced.

A five-year plan becomes a three-year outcome
not because anyone works harder
but because the architecture stops working against itself.

When Vision is aligned, you stop changing direction.
When Value is clear, you stop wasting resources.
When Vehicle is strong, you stop fighting your own model.
When the Pillars are fortified, you stop compensating for weaknesses.
When rhythm is enforced, you stop drifting.

Without these layers, acceleration is impossible.
With them, acceleration is inevitable.

That is why compression works.

Not because of ambition.
Not because of motivation.
Not because of pressure.

Compression works because structure,
when aligned,
moves faster than belief.

A Three-Year Compression Case Study

I often say that compression isn't theory, it's observation.
It's what happens when architecture stops fighting itself.
But nothing illustrates it better than the experience I had with a CEO named Daniel.

Not his real name, of course.
But everything else about the story is real, the struggle, the fear, the breakthroughs, and the quiet moment where a man finally realised he had been living inside a timeline that wasn't true.

When I met Daniel, he was running a £32M technology services company based in Manchester.
A good business.
A proud history.
A tired team.
And a CEO who looked younger than the weight he was carrying.

They wanted to reach £60M in five years.
"Five years" again, the inherited assumption.
A timeline borrowed from committee thinking.
No one could explain why it needed to be five.
It simply sounded sensible.
It sounded realistic.
It sounded responsible.

But architecture does not care about what sounds responsible.
Architecture cares about what is structurally possible.

The moment I walked through their operation, I could see it, not the number, but the drag.
Decision flow was slow.
Responsibility was blurred.
The founder was the emotional centre of gravity.
Teams were exhausted, not because of workload, but because of ambiguity.

This wasn't a company lacking ambition.
This was a company moving through fog.

And fog makes everything take longer.

Year One — Clearing the Fog

The first year of compression is always the same:
a combination of truth-telling, realignment, and structural unburdening.
Daniel didn't like the word "unburdening" at first.
He thought it implied weakness.

But within eight weeks, he understood.

We started with Vision.
Not a slogan.
Not a statement crafted by marketing.
A structural Vision, the destination the architecture was designed to reach.

I'll never forget the moment he realised the Vision they had been using for
years no longer reflected the company they were trying to become.

"It explains everything," he whispered.
"No wonder the team keeps moving sideways."

Next came Value.
Not price.
Not positioning.
Not messaging.
Value, the reason the market chooses you or ignores you.

Their Value had drifted.
Quietly.
Gradually.
Painfully.

Once we sharpened it, decisions suddenly became easier.
The company stopped chasing everything.
They stopped saying yes to projects that diluted them.
They regained relevance.

Then came Vehicle, the operating model.
This was the hardest shift.

"You've outgrown your model," I told him.
"It's too dependent on heroism. Too manual. Too founder-centric. Too slow."

He didn't fight me.
Not because he agreed,
but because he was too tired to disagree.

Once the Vehicle redesign began, the fog lifted.
Flow improved.

The load on Daniel eased.
The team rediscovered competence they had forgotten they had.

By month ten, Daniel said something I only hear when compression is working:

"I feel like the company is no longer pulling me backward."

That is the first milestone of true compression.
Not acceleration.
Not growth.
Release.

By the end of Year One, their revenue had grown from £32M to £38M, not because of strategy, but because friction had been removed.

But the real shift was internal:

Clarity in roles.
Certainty in direction.
Confidence in architecture.

The fog was gone.

Year Two — Releasing Capacity

The second year is where most leaders finally understand what compression feels like.
It feels like momentum without pressure.
Progress without pain.
Speed without strain.

It's the first time they realise:

"We've been working against ourselves all these years."

Daniel's team felt it before he did.
Projects finished faster.
Sales cycles shortened.
Decision-making decentralised.
The founder was no longer the bottleneck.

He walked into one of our quarterly architecture reviews and said,
"Something strange is happening. The company is moving without me."

"Good," I replied.
"That means it's finally scalable."

Then came the moment every compressing organisation faces,

260

the moment where an opportunity arrives sooner than expected.

A global client offered them a contract that would have taken two years to secure in their old world.

Daniel panicked.
"We're not ready for this much work."

"Yes, you are," I said. "Your architecture is. You just haven't fully caught up emotionally."

And I was right.

They delivered the project in a fraction of the expected time because the architecture, not the people, was carrying the burden.

It was also in Year Two that they made a decision that changed everything:

They exited a legacy client that consumed enormous effort but delivered low value.

In the old architecture, that decision would have been unthinkable.
In the new architecture, it was inevitable.

I still remember the CFO's words during our review:

"For the first time, growth feels like less work, not more."

That is compression.

By the end of Year Two, revenue reached £51M, without strain, without chaos, without heroics.

But the number wasn't the real story.

The real story was the leader Daniel was becoming.
He wasn't fighting fires.
He wasn't making every decision.
He wasn't pulled in every direction.
He was becoming the architect.

Year Three — Acceleration Without Pain

The third year is where the magic happens,
not because the company works harder,
but because momentum has accumulated quietly beneath the surface.

When architecture is aligned, acceleration is the natural state.

261

And that's exactly what unfolded.

They entered Year Three with a clarity that felt almost unfair.
Their Vision was sharper.
Their Value was compelling.
Their Vehicle was strong.
Their Pillars were balanced.
Their rhythm was stable.

Every quarter felt like the company taking a deeper breath.

In Month Four, they won a contract that their five-year plan had scheduled for Year Four.
In Month Seven, they expanded into a region that previously felt unreachable.
In Month Nine, a buyer approached them informally, not because they were for sale, but because their structural maturity had become visible.

By the end of Year Three, their revenue reached **£67M**,
surpassing their original five-year target earlier than anyone believed possible.

What took competitors five years
took them thirty-four months.

But numbers don't tell the real story.
Daniel does.

During our final session of that cycle, he said something I'll never forget:

"I spent twenty years believing that growth required sacrifice.
Now I realise that sacrifice is what happens when architecture is wrong."

He paused, looked down at the table, and added:

"We didn't grow faster.
We just stopped moving slower."

That sentence captures compression better than anything I could ever write.

Compression isn't acceleration.
It's the removal of everything that slows a company down.

Once friction disappears,
speed becomes structural.
Progress becomes natural.
Time collapses.

The Lesson Behind the Case Study

When leaders hear this story, they often focus on the numbers.
But the real lesson is this:

Compression is not a miracle. It is a consequence of alignment.

When Vision is clean,
Value is compelling,
Vehicle is capable,
and the Pillars stand strong...

the organisation begins to rise on its own.

You cannot push your way into compression.
You design your way into it.

Daniel's transformation wasn't the result of bravery or brilliance.
It was the result of humility, the willingness to let go of assumptions that no longer served him and the courage to trust the architecture he rebuilt.

Most leaders are closer to compression than they think.
They're not missing capability.
They're missing alignment.

And when alignment arrives,
time bends.

CHAPTER 13:
When to Call a Strategic Architect

The Fear, Instinct, and Gut Tension Before They Call

People believe CEOs call me when they want growth.
They don't.
They call when something inside them stops making sense.

A Strategic Architect is rarely contacted during celebration.
He's called in the quiet tension before something breaks, or just after
something has already started to bend.

For forty years, I've learned to recognise the emotional architecture of that
call long before the phone rings.
It begins as a feeling the leader cannot name.

Not panic.
Not crisis.
Not failure.
Something subtler.

A tightening.
A restlessness.
A whisper of unease behind the confidence.
An instinct they try to ignore, until ignoring it becomes impossible.

Every major engagement I've taken on over the decades began with that
same pattern: a CEO sitting alone somewhere late at night, staring at
numbers that look fine and yet *feel* wrong.

A CEO knows when something doesn't feel right long before they understand
why.

And that gap, between instinct and clarity, is the space where fear begins to
grow.

Where the Tension Really Begins

It rarely starts with a financial problem.
It rarely starts with a market shift.
It rarely starts with a competitor.

It starts with the leader noticing a change in themselves.

They feel heavier.
Not physically, architecturally.
Their decisions take longer.
Their thoughts circle instead of landing.
Their confidence becomes more performative.
Their team meetings feel slightly off.
Their own intuition feels muted, like a radio losing signal.

This is the earliest warning sign of architectural drift:
when the leader's internal clarity erodes before the external indicators reveal anything.

But they don't call at this stage.
Not yet.

Most CEOs tell themselves the same story at first:

"I'm just tired."
"It's just a busy season."
"It will make sense after this quarter."
"We've been here before. It will pass."
"I just need a weekend to reset."

But the unease does not pass.
Because unease is not emotional,
unease is structural.

The leader begins to feel misaligned with their own organisation.
They can't articulate it.
They can't quantify it.
But they can feel it.

And when they can feel it, it doesn't go away.

The Night They Realise Something Is Wrong

There is always a moment, one that most leaders never speak about, where everything becomes quiet enough for the truth to be heard.

It might be during a flight after a board meeting.
It might be alone in a hotel room after a long day of presentations.
It might be sitting in the car outside the house, the engine still running because they're not ready to go inside.
It might be during a routine walk where suddenly the weight becomes undeniable.

he moment varies.
The internal shift does not.

Something in the leader whispers:

"What if I don't understand my organisation as well as I thought?"
"What if I'm missing something important?"
"What if the structure can't support the future I'm aiming for?"
"What if the numbers are lying, or worse, telling a truth I've been avoiding?"

This is the moment fear enters.

Not fear of failure.
Not fear of loss.
Fear of the unknown.

Because leaders don't fear problems.
They fear the problems they cannot see.

And that is when the gut tightens.
That is when the instinct grows sharp.
That is when the leader understands, even if just subconsciously:

"This is bigger than me."

But still, they don't call.

Why Leaders Delay the Call

I've watched CEOs wrestle with this decision more times than I can count.
They delay for one of three reasons:

1. Pride: The Fear of Admitting They Can't See the Fracture

No leader wants to feel blind in their own company.
They've built empires by trusting their instincts, reading the room, sensing danger before anyone else.

So when their own instinct tells them
"something is wrong, but I can't find it,"
it feels like a betrayal.

This is the hardest truth for a high-performer to face:
that their pattern recognition, their most trusted weapon, is no longer enough.

2. Protection: The Fear of Alarming Their Team

A CEO cannot simply walk into the office and say:
"I have a bad feeling. Something's off."

The room would implode.

So they carry the tension alone, shielding others from the drift they cannot yet describe.

This isolation slows them down.
The weight becomes heavier.
And the call becomes closer.

3. Perception: The Fear of Choosing the Wrong Person to Help

Leaders at this level are surrounded by advisors, legal, financial, operational, political.
But advisors deal with symptoms.

A Strategic Architect deals with structure.

And this scares them.
Because the person who sees the truth can also see the leader.

If they choose the wrong person, the consequences are too big.
The cost is too high.
The exposure is too personal.

So they delay.

But delaying only tightens the knot in their stomach.

The Trigger — The Moment They Finally Decide

There is always a moment where hesitation ends.

Sometimes it's a number on a spreadsheet that feels wrong.
Sometimes it's a meeting where everyone nods but no one believes what they're saying.
Sometimes it's a talent leaving unexpectedly.
Sometimes it's customer behaviour shifting without explanation.
Sometimes it's a competitor moving unnaturally fast.

But more often than not, it's something far simpler:

A quiet moment where the leader says,
honestly, privately, without performance:

"I can't keep doing this alone."

That is when they call.

Not because they suddenly understand the fracture.
But because they finally admit they can't see it.

And they need someone who can.

The Call Itself

I can always tell, within the first twenty seconds,
whether a leader is calling because they want help
or because they *need* help.

Wanting help sounds hopeful.
Needing help sounds tired.

The real call, the one that begins the work, doesn't start with strategy.
It begins with confession.

Not emotional confession.
Architectural confession.

"Moe, the numbers are fine, but something feels off."
"Moe, I don't trust my own read of the organisation."
"Moe, the team is strong, but something in the structure doesn't feel right."
"Moe, we're growing, but it doesn't feel sustainable."
"Moe, I can't see the bottleneck, but I know it exists."
"Moe, I feel like I'm fighting my own company."

The words change.
The emotion does not.

It is the same across continents, industries, cultures, and revenue levels.

Behind every one of these sentences is the same truth:

A leader has reached the edge of their own pattern recognition.

And that is where my work begins.

What They Really Want When They Call

They don't want motivation.
They don't want a new strategy.
They don't want a consultant.
They don't want theory.
They don't even want solutions, not at first.

They want clarity.

They want someone who can walk into the room, look at the architecture, and tell them:

What is real.
What is drifting.
What is breaking.
What is possible.
And what must change.

Every CEO who has ever called me, consciously or not, is seeking the same thing:

A second set of eyes that can see the fracture before it becomes visible.

They want to breathe again.
They want the weight to make sense.
They want time to stop feeling like sand slipping through their fingers.
They want control without micromanagement.
They want certainty without arrogance.
They want truth without politics.

Above all, they want their instinct back,
the instinct that built the business in the first place.

The Unspoken Fear Behind the Call

There is something most leaders never tell me,
but I can hear it in the silence between their words:

"What if the fracture is me?"

I never dismiss this fear.
Because sometimes, gently, quietly, it is true.

But the truth is kinder than the fear.

The fracture is rarely the leader.
It is the architecture they've been forced to carry alone.

And the moment they understand this,
their shoulders drop.
Their breathing changes.
Their eyes regain focus.

Because finally, after months or years of quiet tension,
they are no longer alone inside the architecture.

The Ending Truth of This Subchapter

A Strategic Architect is not called when things break.
He is called when the leader senses the break before anyone else can.

Fear brings them to the edge.
Instinct tells them not to ignore it.
Gut tension tells them time is running out.

And then, finally, they pick up the phone.

Not to ask for help.
But to ask for truth.

Because truth, not effort,
is what saves an organisation.

Why Leaders Do Not See the Fracture

People often assume that if a business begins to drift, the CEO must have missed something obvious. They imagine that fractures announce themselves loudly, like cracks in a wall or smoke rising from a fire.

But real fractures, the kind that bring mature companies to crisis, never announce themselves.

They whisper.
They hide.
They camouflage themselves inside success.
 And they emerge only when the structure can no longer carry the load.

Over four decades, I've learned something uncomfortable about leadership:
leaders are usually the last to see the fracture in their organisation.
Not because they lack intelligence.
Not because they lack experience.
But because the architecture is built in such a way that the fracture becomes invisible precisely to the person who needs to see it most.

There are five reasons this happens, none of them rooted in weakness, all of them rooted in structural truth.

1. Leaders Spend Too Much Time at the Altitude Where Problems Disappear

A CEO's perspective is unique, they stand at a height no one else in the organisation stands at.

From that altitude, they see:

the horizon
the competition
the opportunity
the big picture

But altitude has a price.

From high above, cracks look like shadows, not fractures.

They don't look dangerous.
They don't look urgent.
They don't look like something that could collapse the company if ignored.

A CEO once told me, "Moe, everything looks fine from where I sit."
I replied, "That's exactly why it isn't."

Leaders operate in the airspace where symptoms dissolve.
They don't hear the friction in the system.
They don't feel the weight on frontline teams.
They don't experience the hesitation in decision-making or the quiet resentment forming between departments.

The fracture is most visible at ground level,
and ground level is the place leaders are least likely to stand.

2. Success Creates Blind Spots Faster Than Failure

Failure sharpens vision.
Success dulls it.

When things are going well, revenue strong, customers happy, growth steady, the architecture develops soft spots.
Not immediately.
Slowly.
Quietly.

This is when drift begins:

a minor delay
a small misalignment
a slight dip in energy
a whisper of inconsistency

Success convinces leaders of two dangerous lies:

"This is working, so it must be working for the right reasons."
"If it broke, the numbers would show it."

Numbers rarely show architectural fractures until it's too late.

One CEO in Zurich once said to me, "We're growing. What exactly should I be worried about?"

A year later, he knew.
Success had blinded him to the structural fatigue building beneath the surface.

Success is comforting.
Comfort hides fractures.

3. Leaders Trust Effort More Than Architecture

Most CEOs built their companies by relying on effort, their effort, their team's effort, their intuition, their grit.

That bias never truly leaves them.

When something feels wrong, most leaders respond by:

pushing harder
adding more meetings
hiring more people
working longer hours
forcing momentum through willpower

The problem is simple:
effort conceals architectural weakness.

It does not fix it.
It does not reveal it.
It disguises it.

I once told a founder in Dubai, "Your people are compensating for a structural flaw you haven't seen yet."

He frowned.
"What do you mean?"

"They are working so hard, the architecture looks strong from where you sit."

He fell silent. Because he knew it was true.

A company can survive a flawed architecture for years
if enough people bleed to keep it alive.

But eventually the bleeding stops.
And then the fracture appears.

4. The Architecture Protects the Leader From Seeing the Very Thing That Threatens It

Here is something no one tells you:

The higher you rise, the less truth reaches you.

Not because your team hides it maliciously.
They hide it unintentionally, through fear, loyalty, politeness, or simply because they assume you already know.

Employees filter bad news.
Managers soften the truth.
Directors package their concerns into politically safe language.

By the time the information reaches the CEO,
it has been diluted.
Sanitised.
Smoothed.
Optimised.

I once told a board in London, "Your CEO does not have a visibility problem. He has a filtration problem."

Fractures are fragile truths.
They break easily when handled improperly.
And by the time they reach the CEO, they often disappear entirely.

This is why a Strategic Architect must enter the system at ground level, no filter, no politics, no performance.

You cannot fix what you cannot feel.
And leaders often cannot feel the fracture until the architecture becomes unstable.

5. Leaders Become the Counterweight That Hides the Fracture

There is something I've never said publicly, but I've told many CEOs in private:

"You are preventing your own architecture from revealing the truth."

When a leader is strong, decisive, experienced, and intuitive, the organisation begins to lean on them.

This creates a dangerous dynamic, **the founder becomes the glue.**

People use the leader to fill gaps:
When a process is weak, they ask the CEO.
When a role is unclear, they escalate the decision.
When a conflict arises, they wait for direction.
When a department struggles, they rely on the leader's memory, context, or instinct.

And because the leader is competent, everything continues to function.

But competence is not a substitute for architecture.

In the short term, the leader prevents collapse.
In the long term, they prevent detection.

I once told a founder in New York, "Your company is not broken, you are holding it together."

He didn't know whether to thank me or be angry.
Eventually, he understood.

When the leader compensates, the architecture cannot reveal its fracture.
And if the architecture cannot reveal its fracture,
it cannot be repaired.

So Why Don't Leaders See the Fracture?

Because the architecture is designed to conceal it
until it can no longer compensate.
Because success masks it.
Because people soften the truth.
Because effort disguises fragility.
Because the leader's altitude hides ground-level pressure.
Because the leader themselves becomes the stabilising force.

But the deeper truth is this:

Leaders don't see the fracture because they're not supposed to.

A CEO's role is to see the horizon.
A Strategic Architect's role is to see the cracks beneath their feet.

The leader sees the future.
I see the structure that must carry them there.

And when both perspectives come together,
compression begins.

The Ending Truth of This Subchapter

The fracture always exists before the leader notices it.
Not because they failed,
but because the architecture protected them from seeing it.

A company's first fracture is invisible.
Its second fracture is subtle.
Its third fracture is undeniable.

Leaders call me between the second and third.

They feel the tension.
They feel the weight shifting.
They feel the architecture straining.
And instinct, the one thing they still trust, tells them:

"This isn't something I can fix by working harder."

That is when clarity becomes urgent.

Not because the leader is weak.
Because the architecture is speaking.

And finally,
the leader is ready to listen.

Selective Work, Deep Impact

People often ask me why I take on so few clients each year.
They assume it's about time, lifestyle, or the luxury of being selective at this stage of my career.

But the truth is far simpler, and far more structural:

Deep impact requires deep architecture.
And deep architecture cannot be built in shallow relationships.

I learned this decades ago, not from success, but from burnout.

There was a period in my early career where I tried to help everyone.
Large companies, small ones, founders in chaos, leaders in denial, boards in panic, executives who weren't ready to change, teams who wanted transformation without discomfort.

I worked with too many at once.
I carried weight that didn't belong to me.
I tried to save organisations that weren't willing to save themselves.

And the result was predictable.

The work became diluted.
The outcomes became inconsistent.
And I found myself solving the same problems repeatedly for people who had no intention of changing their architecture, only their symptoms.

One evening, after leaving a client office long after midnight, I sat in my car for almost half an hour without turning the key.
Not from exhaustion, but from clarity.

I realised something essential:

Impact doesn't come from helping everyone.
Impact comes from helping the right ones.

Not the richest.
Not the largest.
Not the most visible.
The right ones.

Those who are structurally ready.
Those who are emotionally available.
Those who are humble enough to admit what they cannot see.
Those who understand that architecture, not effort, determines their future.

And those who are willing to work with a level of honesty most leaders spend their entire lives avoiding.

Why Selectivity Is Essential

When people think about selectivity, they imagine exclusivity.
They imagine me filtering based on profile, industry, or revenue.

It has nothing to do with that.

I work with a £30M founder who is hungrier than a £300M founder.
I turn away a £150M CEO who wants cosmetic change instead of structural change.
I say yes to the quiet operator who has built a world-class business but now feels trapped by their own success.

Selectivity is not about scale.
It is about seriousness.

I only work with leaders where the architecture deserves the effort.

Because architecture is heavy work.
It requires trust.
It requires vulnerability.
It requires the willingness to tear down comfortable illusions in order to build structures that can survive pressure.

Most leaders say they want the truth.
Very few are willing to live with it.

The ones who are,
those are the ones I choose.

Why I Only Take On Those Who Can Handle Precision

People underestimate what architectural precision requires.

It demands a level of honesty that can be uncomfortable.
It demands the courage to remove pillars that have sentimental value.
It demands the discipline to adhere to rhythm even when results are strong.
It demands the humility to acknowledge where the leader has become the bottleneck.

I've sat across from CEOs who told me,
"Moe, I want you to be honest, just not about *that*."

And that's when I know they're not ready.

Because structural truth does not negotiate.

When I tell a leader where the fracture is, I expect them to look at it without defence.
I expect them to challenge me, question me, debate me, yes.
But not deny the architecture when it speaks.

The leaders I take on are those who can look at the uncomfortable truth and say:

"Fine. Show me the next step."

Those leaders build companies that scale.
Those leaders compress timelines.
Those leaders evolve.
Those leaders transform.

Precision is not kind.
But it is liberating.

Why Selectivity Protects the Leader and the Organisation

I have seen what happens when a CEO invests deeply in transformation, only to discover the people around them are not willing to evolve with them.

The pain of that realisation is unforgettable.

So when I work closely with a leader, I'm not just evaluating *them*.
I'm evaluating their architecture's capacity to evolve.

Can this team handle the truth?
Can the structure absorb change?
Is the culture strong enough to survive discomfort?
Is the leader protected by rhythm or exposed by chaos?
Are they building for legacy or simply for revenue?

If the architecture is not ready, the work becomes harmful.
Not for me, for them.

A leader who exposes structural truth too early can destabilise their organisation.
A leader who introduces architectural discipline into a culturally fragile environment can create resistance instead of acceleration.

Selective work protects the organisation from premature transformation.

It ensures the architecture bends without breaking.
It ensures the leader grows without destabilising the system.
It ensures outcomes are real, not theoretical.

Why Depth Requires Fewer Relationships

People are often surprised by how selective I am,
six slots per week, one dedicated day, and only when a leader is genuinely
ready.

But depth cannot be industrialised.
Architecture cannot be mass-produced.
Insight cannot be automated.
Transformation cannot be rushed.

When I work with a leader, I enter their architecture.
Not metaphorically, literally.

I walk through their structure.
I feel the pressure points.
I trace decision flows.
I listen for the friction in meetings.
I observe who carries weight and who avoids it.
I watch how the leader responds under pressure.
I study the language the team uses.
I feel the organisation's emotional pulse.

This requires presence.
This requires attention.
This requires availability.

You cannot do deep work with twenty clients at once.
You can barely do it with five.

That is why selectivity is not a luxury.
It is a requirement for impact.

The Paradox of Selective Work

There's a paradox most people miss:

The fewer clients I take, the more powerful the outcomes become.

Because when you go deep,
you see what others miss.
You understand the patterns behind the patterns.
You trace fractures to their origins.
You spot misalignments others never notice.
You feel the architecture changing in real time.

Deep engagement creates deep clarity.
Deep clarity creates deep results.

Selective work is not about scarcity.
It is about intensity.

It is about giving a leader your mind, your instinct, your precision,
and helping them redesign the architecture of their company from the inside
out.

This cannot be done while juggling dozens of relationships.
It can only be done when the work itself becomes a craft.

The Ending Truth of This Subchapter

I'm often described as semi-retired,
but I've never liked the term.
I'm not retired.
I'm refined.

I choose the work that matters.
I choose the leaders who are ready.
I choose the architectures that deserve rebuilding.
I choose the organisations where the truth will be honoured.

Selective work is not about exclusivity.
It is about integrity,
my integrity to the craft,
and the leader's integrity to their own future.

Because when you work deeply with the right leader,
the impact lasts decades.
It shapes families, industries, communities, and legacies.

And that is the only kind of work worth doing.

CHAPTER 14:
Your First Ninety Days of Architectural Change

Your 3XV Reset

There is a moment in every transformation where the leader realises that the next ninety days will define the next nine years.
Not because change requires force,
but because architecture responds best to clarity, and clarity begins with 3XV.

Whenever I begin working with a new CEO, the first thirty days always start the same way:
with a reset they don't yet realise they need.

Most leaders assume their Vision is clear,
their Value is understood,
their Vehicle is capable.

But the moment we begin to examine them structurally,
not emotionally, not narratively, not aspirationally,
the truth begins to surface.

3XV is rarely broken.
It is almost always misaligned.

Misalignment does not scream.
It whispers.
It creates tension in decisions, fatigue in teams, friction in flow, and hesitation in execution.

When 3XV is misaligned, every effort feels heavier.
When it is reset, everything becomes lighter, not because the workload changes, but because the architecture finally stops fighting itself.

The Vision Reset — Seeing the Destination Without Illusion

Vision is often misunderstood as inspiration.
It is not.
Vision is direction.
It is the structural north star of the organisation.
It determines what gets built, who gets hired, which opportunities matter, and which ones become distractions.

But over time, Vision drifts.

Not dramatically, subtly.
It moves through assumptions, market pressures, team dynamics, and the leader's evolving expectations.

When I sit with a CEO and ask,
"Where are you really trying to take this company in the next 3–5 years?"
there is always a pause.

A long one.

Because Vision is the one part of the architecture leaders rarely examine with fresh eyes.
They inherited it.
They outgrew it.
They diluted it.
Or they simply forgot to update it while everything else evolved.

In the first ninety days, we strip Vision down to its structural truth:

What is the real destination?
Not the safe one.
Not the expected one.
The true one.

If the Vision is off by even ten degrees,
the architecture will carry the company miles in the wrong direction.

A Vision reset is not creative.
It is clarifying.

It takes courage to look at the future you actually want
rather than the one you have been pretending to build.

But when Vision is reset correctly, leaders experience something profound:

a sense of internal alignment

a reduction in hesitation
a renewed sense of purpose
a clarity that cuts through noise

The organisation feels it instantly.
Because architecture behaves differently when direction becomes undeniable.

The Value Reset — Why the Market Chooses You or Walks Away

Value drift is one of the most dangerous forms of organisational drift.

Teams feel it before leaders do.
Customers feel it before the numbers show it.
Competitors exploit it long before the board notices it.

Value is not about what you sell.
Value is about why anyone should care.

Value answers the question:

"Why us, not them, and why now?"

Over time, the answer changes,
but most companies don't.

They continue selling what made them relevant five years ago
in a world that no longer rewards that offering.

A Value reset examines three structural questions:

1. Who is our ideal customer today, not historically?
2. What problem do we solve now, not what we used to solve?
3. Why does the market choose us, and is that reason still true?

These questions look simple.
They are not.

They unlock truths leaders often avoid:

that they are serving the wrong customer,
or solving the wrong problem,
or selling the wrong promise,
or competing on a value they themselves no longer believe in.

When we reset Value, we are not adjusting messaging.
We are rebuilding relevance.

And nothing accelerates a company faster than regaining relevance.

Suddenly:

sales cycles shorten
confidence returns
opportunities increase
teams sharpen
decisions simplify

Because clarity in Value eliminates the noise that kept them stuck.

The Vehicle Reset — The Engine That Must Carry Your Future

This is the part that leaders resist the most,
because resetting the Vehicle feels like admitting the model they built is no longer enough.

But this is not weakness.
This is evolution.

A Vehicle is the operating model,
the structure through which the company fulfils its promise.

Every Vision requires a specific type of Vehicle.
If the Vehicle cannot carry the Vision,
the company collapses under the weight of its own ambition.

Most companies begin with a Vehicle built for survival.
Not scale.
Not acceleration.
Not sustainability.

Over time, the leader outgrows their own model.
But they remain loyal to it because it worked in the past.

A Vehicle reset asks:

**Is this model capable of delivering the next stage of growth
without overworking people
or depending on the founder
or breaking under volume
or losing quality
or sacrificing margin?**

When the answer is no,
the reset is unavoidable.

And this is the moment where compression begins,

not because the Vehicle becomes faster,
but because the friction inside the model disappears.

Leaders often describe the same feeling after a Vehicle reset:

"It feels like the company finally started breathing again."

That is the power of architectural alignment.
It gives oxygen back to an organisation that had been gasping for years.

Why the 3XV Reset Must Happen Before Anything Else

Without resetting 3XV, the first ninety days become cosmetic.
Change dissolves.
The Pillars wobble.
Decisions contradict the direction.
Teams become confused.
Execution becomes inconsistent.

But when 3XV is aligned,
truly aligned,
it becomes the coordinates for the entire architecture.

Every system, every hire, every strategy, every target, every rhythm, every Pillar decision
anchors to the same north star.

Resetting 3XV is not about rewriting the business.
It is about revealing the business the leader was meant to build all along.

When Vision becomes clean,
Value becomes sharp,
and the Vehicle becomes capable,
the architecture finally aligns.

And in that alignment
you find the quiet beginning of something extraordinary:

momentum without pressure
progress without force
clarity without confusion
and the first real glimpse
of compression.

Your Pillar Baseline

Once a leader resets 3XV, their Vision, their Value, and their Vehicle, something interesting happens.
They expect momentum.
They expect clarity.
They expect acceleration.
But what comes next is far more important:
a confrontation with reality.

Because the moment 3XV becomes clear, the truth of the Five Pillars reveals itself.
Not the surface-level truth.
Not the "we're doing fine" truth.
The structural truth.

This is why, in the first ninety days, a Pillar Baseline is essential.
Without it, leaders make decisions based on stories, not on architecture.
With it, they finally see what the organisation has been carrying, and what it can no longer carry for them.

A Pillar Baseline is not an audit.
Not a scorecard.
Not a maturity model.
It is a structural MRI, a scan of the load-bearing pillars beneath the company's ambitions.

Why Baselines Matter More Than Targets

Most leaders want to begin with targets:
"We want to reach £X."
"We want to enter this market."
"We want to double our EBITDA."
"We want to scale this division."

Targets are comforting because they feel like progress.
But targets are dangerous when they are built on unstable foundations.

I tell CEOs the same sentence every time:

"Your pace must match the strength of your Pillars."

If Systemisation is weak, speed is dangerous.
If Staffability is weak, growth is expensive.
If Scalability is weak, opportunity becomes strain.
If Sustainability is weak, culture breaks.
If Sellability is weak, valuation collapses.

The Pillar Baseline is the truth-telling moment.
It is where the leader admits, often for the first time, that not all parts of the architecture can support the future at the same speed.

And that's perfectly normal.

What matters is knowing **which** Pillar must be strengthened first.

Systemisation Baseline — Where Flow Holds or Fails

The first thing I look for is not documentation, SOPs, workflows, or technology.

I look for **friction**.

Friction is the enemy of speed.
Friction reveals structural decay.
Friction exposes the gap between effort and architecture.

In the Systemisation baseline, I ask:

- How many decisions bottleneck at the founder or COO?

- How often is work repeated?

- How much time do teams spend clarifying instead of executing?

- How many handoffs require manual oversight or emotional labour?

- Does the organisation run on process or on memory?

This baseline often shocks leaders because they realise something painful:

People are compensating for weak systems, not succeeding because of them.

Once a leader sees this, they stop praising heroics and start eliminating the need for heroics.

Systemisation is not about creating order.
It is about creating flow.
And flow is what makes acceleration sustainable.

Staffability Baseline — Whether the Organisation Can Carry More Weight

This baseline reveals a truth most leaders avoid:

Your people are only as effective as the architecture allows them to be.

If roles are unclear,
if responsibility is chaotic,
if managers are overwhelmed,
if decisions are unclear,
if the founder is the fallback...

no amount of hiring, training, or motivation will fix it.

During the Staffability baseline, I look for:

- Who carries the emotional weight of the company?

- Who makes decisions they shouldn't be making?

- Who avoids decisions entirely?

- Who is exhausted not because of workload but because of ambiguity?

- Where are the cultural fault lines forming?

Most leaders assume they have a people problem.
They do not.
They have an architecture problem showing up in people.

When the Staffability Pillar is weak, the company grows heavier with every customer added.
When it is strong, the company grows lighter.

That is the paradox of Staffability,
clarity reduces effort.

Scalability Baseline — Whether the Vehicle Can Carry Expansion

Scalability is not growth.
Growth is more.
Scalability is *more without strain*.

The Scalability baseline examines:

- Does adding customers create complexity or simplicity?

- Does revenue growth strengthen or stress the system?

- Does the model grow horizontally or vertically?

- Does the leader need to interfere for the business to expand safely?

- Does growth reveal cracks or reinforce structure?

When Scalability is weak:

sales rise,
stress rises faster.

When Scalability is strong:

sales rise,
clarity improves,
costs stabilise,
systems strengthen.

In the baseline, I look for the silent signals, the ones teams feel but never report:

overflowing Slack messages
longer meeting cycles
decisions being pushed upward
quality shifting
delivery timelines slipping
teams firefighting
leaders working late not because they want to, but because the architecture demands it

When Scalability fails, the organisation pretends everything is fine until suddenly, it isn't.
The baseline brings the truth forward long before that moment arrives.

Sustainability Baseline — Whether the Architecture Can Withstand Pressure

People assume sustainability is about wellbeing or culture.
It's not.
It is about **load tolerance**.

How much pressure can the architecture absorb without fracturing?

When I conduct a Sustainability baseline, I'm looking for:

- fatigue that doesn't match workload

- tension between middle management and leadership

- cultural drift

- emotional volatility

- dependency on unofficial leaders

- avoidance of difficult conversations

- anything the team hides from the CEO

Sustainability is the invisible Pillar.
When it is weak, companies accelerate beautifully,
and then collapse suddenly.

When it is strong, companies absorb impact without losing rhythm.

Leaders often underestimate this baseline because they cannot quantify emotional load.

But architecture feels emotional load before it feels operational load.
A team under chronic structural pressure becomes a team incapable of supporting acceleration.

Sellability Baseline — Whether the Company Is Transferable

This baseline has nothing to do with selling the company.

It has everything to do with **building a company that can grow without being held together by the founder's memory, instinct, and involvement.**

During the Sellability baseline, I ask:

- If the founder left for 90 days, what breaks?

- Where is knowledge trapped in people rather than systems?

- Which decisions are undocumented but culturally assumed?

- Which relationships are founder-dependent?

- Which roles exist only because the architecture is flawed?

Leaders often react strongly to this baseline.
Some feel confronted.
Some feel relieved.
All feel exposed.

Because this baseline reveals the truth:

**transferability is maturity,
and maturity accelerates growth.**

A company that cannot be transferred cannot be compressed.
A company that *can* be transferred scales without resistance.

The Real Purpose of the Pillar Baseline

The Pillar Baseline is not designed to make you feel good.
It is designed to make you feel clear.

Because clarity is the precursor to acceleration.
Confusion is the precursor to collapse.

Once a leader sees the baseline of all five Pillars,
their strengths, their weaknesses, their fractures, their opportunities,
they can finally answer the most important architectural question:

"Which Pillar must I strengthen first?"

Not second.
Not third.
Not eventually.

First.

This is the heart of the first ninety days:

not trying to fix everything,
but choosing the right place to begin.

Strengthen the wrong Pillar,
and the architecture resists.
Strengthen the right Pillar,
and the entire structure rises with it.

The Quiet Ending Truth

Most leaders spend years trying to grow without ever understanding the
structure carrying them.

The Pillar Baseline is the moment the structure speaks.

It shows leaders what their team already feels.
It reveals what their numbers have been hiding.
It exposes what their instinct has been whispering.
And it clarifies the path that will finally lead to acceleration.

Because architecture does not require perfection.
It requires truth.

And truth, when applied correctly,
is what turns five-year ambitions
into three-year outcomes.

Your First Structural Move

Insight

First Structural Move

There is a moment in every leader's journey where the truth becomes unavoidable.
Not because something dramatic happens,
not because a crisis erupts,
not even because thc numbers turn against them,
but because clarity removes the luxury of pretending.

After you complete your 3XV reset
and confront the Pillar Baseline,
you arrive at one of the most important crossroads of the entire ninety-day transformation:

Your first structural move.

It is the moment you decide not only *what* must change,

but *where* you will place your weight as a leader.

Your first structural move is never cosmetic.
It is never symbolic.
It is never small.

It is the intervention that tells the entire organisation, quietly and unequivocally:

"This time we are not adjusting, we are redesigning."

And that is why your first move matters more than your next ten moves combined.

The Weight of the First Move

Leaders underestimate how watched they are in this phase.
Teams don't need an announcement.
They don't need a speech.
They don't need a roadmap.

They watch a single thing:

Where does the leader place their attention first?

Because your first structural move communicates your true priorities more honestly than any strategy deck ever could.

If you choose the wrong place,
the architecture hesitates.
People hesitate.
Momentum hesitates.

But when you choose correctly,
a subtle shift moves through the entire organisation.

Meetings change tone.
Managers breathe differently.
People lift their heads more often.
Decision flow strengthens.
Ownership begins to rise.

Not because you've done much,
but because the organisation feels that the architecture is finally being taken seriously.

Why the First Move Is Almost Always Harder Than It Should Be

I've watched hundreds of leaders make their first structural move.
Some do it quietly.
Some do it reluctantly.
Some do it with fire in their eyes.
But all of them share the same internal turbulence:

They know that their first move must disrupt something familiar.

That familiarity might be a person,
a process,
a norm,
a habit,
a belief,
or a long-standing pattern that has kept the company "comfortable" but fundamentally unscalable.

Your first move forces you to confront one uncomfortable reality:

You cannot redesign architecture without destabilising the parts of the business that relied on the old one.

That destabilisation is not chaos,
it is renewal.

But it feels uncomfortable, so leaders often hesitate.
They wait for the "perfect timing."
They wait for more certainty.
They wait for validation, reassurance, or consensus.

Architecture punishes hesitation.

Because while you wait,
the organisation watches,
and the architecture interprets silence as resistance.

Your first move is the moment you break that silence.

How You Know Which Move Must Come First

It's rarely the move that feels the most urgent.
Urgency is emotional.
Architecture is structural.

In the first ninety days, your true first intervention becomes clear through a pattern of recognition you cannot unsee:

Where is the organisation leaking the most energy?
Where is the architecture carrying weight it cannot sustain?
Where is the drift accumulating fastest?
Where does the team feel most confused or unsupported?
Which Pillar destabilises the others?

You already felt it during your baseline.
You sensed it in meetings.
You noticed it in conversations.
Your instinct highlighted it long before your framework confirmed it.

Every company has a "ground zero",
the place where pressure concentrates,
where behaviour becomes inconsistent,
where decisions slow down,
where accountability dissolves,
where opportunity gets lost,
where the architecture begins to fail.

That is where the first structural move must occur.

Not because it is the biggest problem,
but because it is the **load-bearing fracture**.

Fixing it stabilises the entire system.
Ignoring it destabilises everything else.

The First Move Is Always a Message

Your first structural move reshapes the emotional architecture of the organisation as much as the operational one.

When a CEO moves decisively on the right structural issue, it sends a message that echoes through every corridor of the business:

"We will not tolerate drift."
"We will not rely on heroics."
"We are building for the future, not surviving the past."
"We are no longer guessing, we are architecting."

"We are aligning structure with ambition."
"We are taking this seriously."

Teams don't respond to slogans.
They respond to actions.
The first structural move is the action that converts your architecture from an idea into a commitment.

A Story From the Field

Several years ago, I worked with a CEO whose organisation had grown to £80M with impressive momentum, on paper.
But beneath the surface, you could feel the drag:
decision bottlenecks,
middle-management fatigue,
inconsistent delivery,
and a founder overwhelmed by being the only stabilising force.

During the Pillar Baseline, it became obvious:
Systemisation was collapsing under the weight of informal decision-making.

Everything felt urgent.
Everything felt heavy.
Everything felt founder-dependent.

When I asked him to choose his first structural move, he hesitated.

"I feel like we should start with people," he said.
"No," I replied. "Your people are exhausted because your structure is exhausted. Strengthen the structure, and your people will become strong again."

His first move was deceptively simple:
he created a decision-flow redesign and removed himself from six types of decisions he had been making for years.

Within two weeks, the entire company breathed differently.

Within two months, the architecture stabilised.

Within six months, the company regained momentum and began scaling into markets they had avoided for years.

And it all began with one structural move.

Why the First Move Feels Smaller Than It Actually Is

Your first structural move will often look modest from the outside:

reshaping a process,
clarifying a decision owner,
removing a bottleneck,
ending a legacy behaviour,
realigning roles,
redefining priorities,
introducing new meeting rhythms,
or strengthening a single Pillar.

But structurally, it represents something far larger:

You are changing the load path inside your organisation.

You are redistributing weight.
You are removing pressure from the wrong places.
You are strengthening a pillar that was quietly failing.
You are redirecting flow toward stability.
You are restoring alignment that had been absent for years.

The move may be small.
The consequence never is.

The Internal Transformation You Will Feel

Your first structural move changes you as much as the organisation.

It forces you to shift from operator to architect.
From firefighter to designer.
From doing to shaping.
From reacting to orchestrating.

Leaders often describe the same sensation after making their first structural move:

"It feels like I'm finally running the business again, instead of letting the business run me."

There is a clarity that arrives,
a calmness that wasn't there before,
a sense of direction that was previously swallowed by noise.

Your first structural move is a reclaiming.
Not of power,
but of stewardship.

The Ending Truth

The first structural move is not the beginning of change,
it is the beginning of transformation.

It tells the organisation,
and more importantly, yourself:

**"We are no longer living by accident.
We are building by design."**

And once that move is made,
the architecture responds.
The Pillars strengthen.
The drift slows.
The fog lifts.
Momentum returns.
And the next ninety days stop being a plan,
they become a turning point.

A Personal Request From the Author

If you've journeyed with me through these pages, thank you.

Not as an author thanking a reader,
but as one leader acknowledging another who chose to step into deeper clarity,
greater honesty,
and a higher standard of leadership.

Books like this don't spread because of algorithms or advertising.
They spread because of leaders like you,
leaders who recognise truth when they see it
and are willing to share it with others who need it.

If this book helped you see your organisation more clearly…
If a story stayed with you…
If a single line shifted your thinking, even slightly…
then I have one sincere request:

Would you leave a review on Amazon?

Your perspective matters more than you think.

Your words, even a few sentences, help other leaders decide
whether this book will meet them at the moment they need it most.

Reviews are the oxygen of this work.
They tell me what served you.
They shape what I create next.
And they help this book reach leaders who may be facing the same pressures
you were facing when you opened these pages.

If you feel moved to go further, you might also:

• share a quote or insight on LinkedIn
• write a short reflection or blog post
• mention the chapter that hit you the hardest
• or simply tell another leader why this book mattered to you

Every review, every post, every share expands the circle of leaders who can benefit from the architecture we've explored together.

You gave your time to read this book.
That alone is an honour.
If you choose to share your experience publicly,
you will help the next leader find the clarity they've been searching for.

Thank you, sincerely, for reading, reflecting, and for walking this journey with me.
Your review means more than you know.

Moe Nawaz

www.ingramcontent.com/pod-product-compliance
Lightning Source LLC
Chambersburg PA
CBHW071445220526
45472CB00003B/679